CHRISTIAN STUDIES II

The Rise and Fall of Israel and the Period of the Prophets

Teacher Manual

Cheryl Lowe & Leigh Lowe

MEMORIA PRESS

MEMORIA PRESS
www.MemoriaPress.com

CHRISTIAN STUDIES II
The Rise and Fall of Israel and the Period of the Prophets

TEACHER MANUAL
Cheryl Lowe & Leigh Lowe

ISBN 978-1-61538-737-3

Second Edition © 2016 Memoria Press | 0321

CONTENTS

BOOKS OF THE OLD TESTAMENT

Law   5

Genesis	Book of Beginnings
Exodus	Deliverance from Egyptian Bondage
Leviticus	Book of the Law
Numbers	Wilderness Wanderings
Deuteronomy	Second Book of the Law

History   12

Joshua	Conquest of Canaan
Judges	No King in Israel
Ruth	The Great Grandmother of David
I II Samuel	Saul and David
I II Kings	Solomon and the Divided Kingdom
I II Chronicles	The Southern Kingdom of Judah
Ezra	The Jews Return to Jerusalem
Nehemiah	The Cupbearer of Xerxes Visits Jerusalem
Esther	A Jewish Queen in the Persian Court

Wisdom   5

Job	The Patience and Suffering of Job
Psalms	The Song Book of Israel
Proverbs	Wise Sayings for Daily Living
Ecclesiastes	All is Vanity
Song of Solomon	A Wedding Love Song

Major Prophets   5

Isaiah	A Prophet for Judah
Jeremiah	A Religion of the Heart
Lamentations	Laments for the Fall of Jerusalem
Ezekiel	Dry Bones
Daniel	Visions, Dreams, and Daniel in the Lion's Den

Minor Prophets   12

Prophets to Israel and Judah

Hosea	An Unfaithful Wife Symbolizes Unfaithful Israel
Joel	The Day of the Lord Is Coming for Judah
Amos	God Requires Justice and Righteousness
Obadiah	God's Judgment on Edom
Jonah	A Mission to Nineveh and Three Days in a Whale

Prophets to Judah

Micah	Judgment for Israel & Judah; Future Glory for Little Bethlehem
Nahum	God's Judgment on Nineveh
Habakkuk	God Will Use Babylon to Punish the Wickedness of Judah
Zephaniah	The Day of the Lord Is Coming for Judah and the Nations

Postexilic Prophets

Haggai	A Call to Rebuild the Temple
Zechariah	Rebuild the Temple, the Messiah Is Coming
Malachi	A Final Warning, the Day of the Lord Will Come

Deuterocanonical Books*   7

Tobit	A Family is Blessed by Their Faithfulness to the Lord
Judith	The Lord Delivers Israel from Attack
I Maccabees	Judas Maccabeus Leads Revolt to Free Israel from Greek Rule
II Maccabees	A More Detailed Look at a Short Period within the Maccabean Revolt
Wisdom	Seek Justice and Wisdom
Sirach	The Beginning of Wisdom is Fear of the Lord
Baruch	The Trauma of Exile: Sin, Punishment, Repentance, Return

*The "deuterocanonical" books, most likely written in Aramaic, are included in Catholic and Eastern Orthodox Bibles. These books are found in historic Bibles such as the Greek Septuagint and the Latin Vulgate, and even though they are considered apocryphal (disputed) by Protestants, they are important documents for the study of Israel and the church; for this reason, students should learn them. Latin students will encounter the deuterocanon when they begin Latin translation with the Vulgate.

INTRODUCTION

What is Christian Studies?

In essence, Christian Studies is a means of educating our children in the most magnificent and meaningful story ever told—the Bible. For this task, both the substance and form have been selected carefully for this study. What is the substance of Christian Studies?

Beyond all other sacred or religious texts, the Bible contains the crucial narrative for all human history. Thus, more than just a great story, it is *the* story! Uniquely more than a mere book, the Bible remains God's personal self-disclosure of His will and ways to the world He created. From the first glorious moments in the Garden of Eden to the arresting visions of Saint John in Revelation, God has been calling out a people to bear His name. In following the story of that rescued people, we find the Salvation History of God, the story of redemption. The ultimate significance of Salvation History, however, is not found merely in the individual stories along the way, but rather in the amazing way the stories link together. In this way, we desire to tell *God's story* through the stories of Abraham, Moses, or David.

Therefore, to preserve the unity of the story, it is fitting that our students should encounter the text of the Bible in the storybook form of *The Golden Children's Bible*. We feel that we have found in *The Golden Children's Bible* the closest, most appropriate resource for the actual text of Scripture. We appreciate the fact that *The Golden Children's Bible* was based on the King James Bible, because the King James Bible is the poetic and literary version of Scripture and a necessary preparation for the study of English literature, as well as a foundation for a deep spiritual life. The pictures in *The Golden Children's Bible* are also significant as a teaching tool, and this dignified presentation preserves the reverence we want our students to maintain for the stories of the Bible, distinct from other stories they may have read. Then, what is the format of this study?

With every story, the wonder and awe of the experience depends upon how well the story is told. More than any other tales, these stories can bring about deep spiritual enrichment. How much more should we strive to engage the hearts and imaginations of our students when we tell the story of God's dealings with mankind? We have made it our goal to avoid trite, simplistic presentations of these magnificent stories. Rather, our task is to communicate effectively both the complexity and breadth of God's Salvation History. How can our students experience a deep sense of awe at the appearance of Jesus Christ, the fulfillment of all of God's promises, unless they feel the Old Testament groans of expectation and longing, such as those found in the period of the Judges or during the Exile? Therefore, we have developed this curriculum for that type of careful narrative approach. Each lesson contains the following:

a. Facts to Know—the important names and terms for each story

b. Memory Verse—a verse that represents well the essence of the lesson's teaching

c. Comprehension Questions—the means of solidifying understanding of the story's basic details

d. Geography—Students will use the Unit Maps located at the end of each Unit in the Student Workbook to locate important locations from each lesson and from Biblical History.

e. Activities (not in Student Book)—additional helps for comprehending the most important information for the lesson

Also, the Teacher Guide often includes additional geography, timelines, cumulative memory work, and discussion questions for each lesson. All of these features help the teacher offer the student a fuller engagement with this most important story. To that end, we have included a Background and Summary section for each lesson to aid the teacher in understanding the each story and its essential teachings.

In sum, we believe that our Christian Studies series provides students with a solid foundation of biblical knowledge that parents can use in shaping the religious character of their children. For our families, we hope to see young lives enriched by spiritual truths and formed in Christlike character through their progress in this study. Teachers, students, and parents, enjoy the wonder and majesty of God's unfolding story.

TEACHING GUIDELINES

- **Facts to Know** — For each lesson, we have identified the most important names, dates, places, terms, or phrases from the story. The teacher should review these important items and define them within the context of the story. Use the Facts to Know section for drill work, recitation, or quizzes. These are the most important ideas for the lesson and should be the focus of discussion.
- **Memory Verse** — Because memorization is a lost art, parents and teachers today rarely have a vision for the quantity and quality of Scripture that children can and should commit to memory. We have selected passages that should lead the student into a love and appreciation for Scripture and its teaching while at the same time offering them an opportunity to reflect on the deeper truths of the lesson. The student should spend the week committing the lesson's verse to memory, and the teacher should offer the student recitation opportunities later in the week.
- In addition to the memory verses that coincide with *The Golden Children's Bible* (GCB), the students will also review their memory verses from the Copybooks. The goal is for students to memorize and retain all of the Scripture they have learned over the course of their schooling. Throughout *Christian Studies I, II,* and *III*, the students will be directed to review verses from a master list in the back of the book. Students should be able to recite all of the Scripture from the current year in addition to verses from previous years.
- **Comprehension Questions** — These questions focus on the most important details from the lesson's story. The answers provided in the Teacher Guide may sometimes provide more information than the student needs to include in his or her answer.
- **Geography** — Students will locate important places from each lesson and from Biblical History on the maps located at the end of each Unit. A knowledge of the relative locations of important events and of the movements of the people in each lesson will give students a fuller understanding of the Bible stories they are studying.
- **Activities (Teacher Guide only)** — This section includes picture reviews ("Picturing the Truth"), geography, timelines, and family trees. The picture review should be done orally. These additional exercises will help solidify in the student's mind the most important features of the story and reinforce the big picture of Salvation History.
- **Review Lessons** — Designed to promote mastery of the content covered, the review lessons test the student's recall of the most important information in the preceding five lessons. Students should work through the Review Lessons with the teacher as a preparation for the unit tests, available in the back of this book.

THE TEACHING SCHEDULE

Day One:

- Read the *Golden Children's Bible* selection. Because of the rich language, two readings are recommended. Ask students to pre-read the *Golden Children's Bible* selection and then also read it aloud together in class. Discuss challenging vocabulary in context as you read. Summarize the story, put it in context, and make sure students understand the central topic. Introduce the Memory Verse and discuss why this particular verse was chosen for the lesson. (30 min.)

Day Two:

- The Facts to Know section prioritizes the information a student will remember for a lifetime. Discuss each fact thoroughly. If the fact is a location, point it out on a map or globe. If a person, discuss all that is known about him. For example, Isaac is described as Abraham and Sarah's son. Do students remember Abraham and Sarah? What were their previous names? Why was the name Isaac chosen?

- Drill the Facts to Know for each lesson and include a weekly cumulative review of all Facts to Know in the Christian Studies sequence. The Facts to Know section is also the best source for supplemental Copybook exercises. (20 min.)

Day Three:

- Master the Memory Verse for the lesson and review all previously learned Scripture from the Memoria Press Copybooks as well as those in this Christian Studies series. Use the Disappearing Line Technique to teach the new verse. Do not ask students to memorize it independently. Recite the whole verse together several times. Break the verse down into small sections. Have students recite one section together, and then erase that section. Pointing to the "erased" section on the board, ask students individually and then in unison, to recite what you erased. Repeat until the whole verse has been erased from the board. As a final exercise, students should stand and recite the verse independently with poise and perfection. (20-30 min.)

Day Four:

- Complete Comprehension Questions. Discuss each question thoroughly. Compose a sentence with the student that offers the best, most complete answer. Do not underestimate this opportunity to practice grammar, spelling, punctuation, and composition. Students should not write one-word or incomplete answers. (30 min.)

Day Five:

- Complete the Geography activity in the Student Workbook, as well as the Activities in the Teacher Guide, which offer picture reviews (orally), geography lessons, timelines, and exercises that reinforce the lesson. This is the time to hold Vocabulary Bees, Facts to Know Drills, or cumulative Memory Verse Recitations. Any supplemental art, geography, or research activities can be added now. This is also the time to test or quiz students on the lesson. (20-30 min.)

LESSON 1

BACKGROUND AND SUMMARY

Moses has seen the Promised Land from Mount Nebo, but does not enter it. Instead, before he dies, he tells the people that Joshua will be their new leader. The 40 years of wandering in the wilderness are at an end, and the Israelites may now enter into Canaan. And so, The Rise of Israel begins here, just outside of the borders of Canaan, near the southeast side of the Jordan River.

At this time in history, Canaan was an area in the Middle East with many powerful cities and kingdoms. Joshua and the Israelites had to face these Canaanite peoples in order to win the Promised Land. The first city and kingdom to conquer was Jericho. The story of Jericho's Fall follows this basic order of events:

- Joshua sends two spies to the land.
- The spies lodge at Rahab's house.
- Jericho's king is aware of the spies, and commands Rahab to bring them out, but Rahab hides them.
- The spies promise to spare Rahab and her family because of her help.
- Joshua crosses the Jordan River and marches with the Ark around the city 7 days; on the last day, at the sound of shouts and horns, the walls fall and Jericho is taken.
- Rahab and her family are spared.

FACTS TO KNOW

1. **Joshua**: followed after Moses to lead the Israelites in the Conquest of Canaan
2. **Canaan**: Promised Land of Israelites; also known as Israel, Palestine, or the Holy Land
3. **Jordan River**: river that Israel crossed through to enter the Promised Land
4. **Rahab the harlot**: hid the spies sent into Jericho
5. **Jericho**: first city to be conquered by Israel in Canaan
6. **flax**: plant; produces linseed oil; linen fabric made from fibers

MEMORY VERSE

> #### JOSHUA 1:9
> *Have not I commanded thee? Be strong and of a good courage; be not afraid, neither be thou dismayed: for the Lord thy God is with thee whithersoever thou goest.*

1. What does it mean to be "of a good courage"?
   to be brave and show no fear

2. What does "whithersoever thou goest" mean?
   wherever they would go

3. What reason do the Israelites have to not be afraid?
   God had promised to be with them always.

VOCABULARY AND EXPRESSIONS

1. **"our hearts melted"**: This is not a romantic expression; rather, it describes utter fright and terror. When they heard what God was doing for the Israelites, the Canaanites had faint hearts.

2. **parapet**: a wall, rampart, or elevation to protect soldiers (from Latin *parare* + *pectus*, "breast-high defense")

3. **spoils**: goods and riches taken in war

GEOGRAPHY (FOR ALL LESSONS)

To orient students to the locations listed, first help them find the Eastern Hemisphere, Mediterranean Sea, and Israel on both a globe and a world map. Always go back and forth between a globe, world map, and smaller local map, so that students learn the specific locations for each lesson in relationship to the surrounding area.

COMPREHENSION QUESTIONS

1. What was the arrangement Rahab made with the spies? <u>Rahab promised not to tell the king</u> <u>about the spies if they would save her family. (p. 179)</u>

2. How did Rahab mark her father's house? <u>She tied a piece of scarlet cord in the window.</u> <u>(p. 181)</u>

3. What does "faint with fear" mean? <u>It means extremely afraid, weak with fear. (p. 181)</u>

4. Why were the people of Jericho so afraid of Israel? <u>The people of Jericho had received word</u> <u>about how God had brought Israel out of Egypt with mighty acts of power. (p. 179)</u>

5. What orders did Joshua give the priests? Describe their procession around the city. <u>"Take up the ark</u> <u>of the covenant and let seven priests carrying seven trumpets of rams' horns march</u> <u>before the ark of the Lord." The priests were guarded by armed men in front and</u> <u>behind. (p. 183)</u>

6. What orders did Joshua give the Israelites? How many days did they march? <u>"Surround the city,</u> <u>and let those that are armed march before the ark of the Lord." They marched for seven</u> <u>days. (p. 183)</u>

GEOGRAPHY

1. Locate on your map and memorize:
   - ☐ Mt. Nebo
   - ☐ Jordan River
   - ☐ Jericho

BIG PICTURE OF THE BIBLE

Read the following verses and then pose the discussion questions to your students.

- **Deuteronomy 7:17-26:** How does Moses say the Lord will lead the conquest of Canaan?
- **Mark 1:9:** What is the significance of the Jordan River in Jesus' earthly ministry? How does it relate to the story?
- **Hebrews 11:30:** What is the role that Israel's faith played in the conquest of Jericho?
- **Matthew 1:5:** Whose name do you recognize in this list? Why is it significant, and what does it tell us about Jesus?

MEMORY WORK

Use a chalk or dry-erase board to help the students start to memorize the first five books of the Bible, or Pentateuch.

1. Genesis
2. Exodus
3. Leviticus
4. Numbers
5. Deuteronomy

GEOGRAPHY

Invasion of Canaan / Fall of Jericho:

- **Mt. Nebo** is where Moses died.
- Joshua sent spies to **Jericho** from the east side of the **Jordan** near **Mt. Nebo**.

ACTIVITIES

- p. 180: Identify the spies. Who is helping them down from the roof? Rahab
- p. 182: In which city does the story take place? Find it on the map. Jericho
- p. 183: Describe what is happening in the picture. What are the men carrying? What are their trumpets made of? The Levites are carrying rams' horns as they march around the city.
- pp. 184-185: Who is standing before the Israelite army? What has happened to the walls of Jericho? Joshua. They fell at the sound of the trumpets and horns blowing and the people shouting.
- pp. 140-143: Review the Ark of the Covenant and the articles of Old Testament worship.
- Draw a picture of the Israelites marching around the city with their horns.

LESSON 2

BACKGROUND AND SUMMARY

Between the Fall of Jericho and our story, the Israelites hit a snag in their conquest. One of them, named Achan, had taken some of the spoils from Jericho that had been banned. Because of Achan's sin, Israel was at first defeated by the men of Ai. For a moment the tides had turned and now it was the hearts of the Israelites that melted before their enemies. Once the sin was punished, however, the Lord forgave Israel and fought for them again. The story of this lesson is as follows:

- God fights for Israel and they defeat Ai; all the cities of Jordan (except Gibeon) are afraid and join together to fight Israel.

- Messengers from Gibeon trick Joshua by appearing as distant people in order to solicit a peace treaty.

- Joshua discovers Gibeon's trick, and they become slaves of Israel.

- The Kings of the Amorites lay siege to Gibeon. Israel defeats the Amorites because the Lord fights for them with hailstones; Joshua commands the sun to stop so all the enemies can be pursued.

- After the land is conquered and divided among Israel, Joshua urges the tribes not to become friends with any survivors of the defeated nations; Joshua dies.

- Israel associates with idolators; they are oppressed by kings, including Jabin. Deborah and Barak deliver Israel, and Sisera, Jabin's great captain, is killed by Jael, fulfilling Deborah's prophecy.

LESSON 2: Joshua and the Hivites | The Slaying of Sisera
Golden Children's Bible: pp. 186-191 (Joshua 8-11, 23-24; Judges 4-5)

FACTS TO KNOW

1. **Ai**: second city of Canaan conquered by the Israelites
2. **Gibeon**: rich city of Canaan that tricked Joshua
3. **Hivites**: rich and wily people of Gibeon
4. **Amorites**: allied with the king of Jerusalem against Joshua
5. **Valley of Ajalon**: where Joshua fought the Amorites
6. **Sisera**: captain of the army of Jabin, King of Canaan
7. **Deborah**: female judge of the Israelites; defeated Sisera; prophesied about the defeat of the Canaanites
8. **Barak**: general of the Israelites

MEMORY VERSE

> **JOSHUA 10:12**
> *Sun, stand thou still upon Gibeon and thou, Moon, in the valley of Ajalon.*

1. Who is speaking in the verse?
   Joshua

2. What request does Joshua make?
   He asked God to hold the sun steady in the sky and postpone sunset.

3. Why does Joshua make this request of the Lord?
   The Israelite army needed more daylight to finish winning the battle with their enemies.

VOCABULARY AND EXPRESSIONS

1. **"hewers of wood, drawers of water"**: bondsmen, simple workers or slaves

2. **booty**: spoils, loot, plunder

3. **wineskins**: bags made of animal skin, such as goat, used for holding wine; can only be filled once

4. **"waxed old and stricken in age"**: Suffering from the effects of old age, Joshua spoke at length to the people.

5. **avenge**: to inflict punishment in return for harm done

6. **expel**: to banish or force out

COMPREHENSION QUESTIONS

1. The people of Gibeon are described as "rich and wily" men. How were the men wily? How did Joshua curse them? __Wily means devious and clever. They presented themselves as poor men from a distant land in order to trick Joshua into giving them a promise of peace. When he learned the truth, Joshua cursed them to remain servants of Israel. (p. 187)__

2. How did God assist Joshua in the battles with the Amorites? __God stopped the sun and moon so that Joshua's forces could finish the fighting. (p. 188)__

3. What were Joshua's final instructions to the Israelites? How old was Joshua when he died? __Joshua commanded the Israelites to remember the word of the Lord: obey the law of Moses, do not pray to or serve the gods of the land. (p. 189) Joshua was 110 years old when he died. (p. 189)__

4. Who oppressed the people of Israel for twenty years in the land? __Sisera (p. 190)__

5. How did the Lord give Israel victory over Jabin and Sisera? __The Lord promised to sell Sisera into the hands of a woman. Barak met Sisera in battle at Mt. Tabor, but Sisera escaped and fled to Kedesh, where she rested in the tent of Jael and killed him. (p. 190)__

6. What was the positive outcome of Jabin's defeat? __Israel enjoyed 40 years of peace in Canaan. (p. 190)__

GEOGRAPHY

1. Locate on your map and memorize the locations of these important battles:

   ☐ Gibeon   ☐ Kedesh   ☐ Ajalon   ☐ Ai

BIG PICTURE OF THE BIBLE

Read the following verses and then pose the discussion questions to your students.

- **Deuteronomy 30:15-20:** What do Moses' final words warn the people not to do?
- **Mark 3:13-19:** What is significant about the number of disciples that Jesus chooses? How does it relate to our story?

MEMORY WORK

Use a chalk or dry-erase board to help the students continue to memorize the first five books of the Bible, or Pentateuch.

1. Genesis
2. Exodus
3. Leviticus
4. Numbers
5. Deuteronomy

GEOGRAPHY

Joshua and the Hivites:

- Gilgal is a few miles N of **Jericho**.
- The Amorites occupied the land east and west of the **Jordan**.
- Joshua is buried about 20 miles SW of **Shechem**.

Slaying of Sisera:

- Mt. Tabor is near the **Jezreel** valley.

ACTIVITIES

- pp. 186-187: Find Joshua. What are the Hivites doing in the picture?
  The Hivites are begging Joshua for a promise of peace.

- pp. 188-189: Who is hiding in the cave? What is happening to the people outside?
  The kings of the Amorites are hiding in a cave while they watch the hail kill their soldiers.

- p. 191: Who is the man resting in the tent? Who is the woman with the bowl of milk?
  Sisera is resting in Jael's tent while she offers him some milk.

LESSON 3

BACKGROUND AND SUMMARY

During the four-hundred-year period between the death of Joshua and the rise of Israel's first king, Israel was led by the Judges. Often military leaders, the Judges served as generals, prophets, and priests for the people. The Book of Judges chronicles the series of repeated covenant failures that characterized that portion of Israel's history.

Found seven times in the text, the Old Testament relates those failures with the expression "And the children of Israel did evil in the sight of the Lord." Thus, a cycle began for the people in which a) God removed the covenant blessings, b) Israel received disaster at the hands of the nations, c) Israel repented and prayed to God, d) God delivered the people through a judge, e) the return of blessing was followed by renewed pride, and the cycle repeated itself. The next few lessons showcase the ups and downs of Israel's cycle of sin.

The story of this lesson is as follows:

- Midian oppresses Israel 7 years.
- An angel visits Gideon and sends him to save Israel from Midian.
- He destroys Baal's altars at night.
- Midian and Amalek encamp at Jezreel, many miles north.
- Gideon gathers men, gets two signs with fleece of God's intent.
- Gideon pares army down to 300 men (fearing & non-lapping leave).
- Spying on the camp, Gideon rejoices at the dream of a soldier.
- Divides men in three companies with trumpets and jars with lights; they attack the camp and win. Forty years of peace for Israel follow.
- Abimelech kills all the sons of Gideon except Jotham, who escapes.
- Jotham tells parable of the bramble on Mt. Gerizim to men of Shechem, which turns out as a prophecy: Abimelech later destroys the men of Shechem due to a quarrel, and he is killed while besieging a tower in Thebez.

FACTS TO KNOW

1. **Midianites**: ruled the Israelites for seven years; defeated by Gideon
2. **Gideon**: called by the Lord to defeat Midian with 300 men
3. **Yahweh-Shalom**: altar to the Lord in Ophrah, means "the Lord is peace"
4. **Jotham**: Gideon's youngest son; told parable of the bramble
5. **Abimelech**: Gideon's son; his death fulfilled Jotham's parable of the bramble
6. **Baal**: a false god of the Canaanites
7. **bramble**: thorny bush; not valuable

MEMORY VERSE

> **JUDGES 6:1**
>
> *And the children of Israel did evil in the sight of the Lord: and the Lord delivered them into the hand of Midian seven years.*

1. How have the children of Israel done evil in the sight of the Lord?
   The people have forgotten the warnings of both Moses and Joshua and turned to serve the gods of the land (i.e., the Baals).

2. What does "delivered them into the hand of Midian" mean?
   God gave Midian opportunity to take control over the Israelites.

3. Why do the people not yet have possession of the Promised Land though they have already arrived?
   They have not yet learned how to serve God alone. (See Judges 2:11, 4:1, and 13:1.)

VOCABULARY AND EXPRESSIONS

1. **"threshing wheat"**: separating the seed from the harvested plant
2. **"Yahweh-Shalom"** (ya **way** sha **lowm**): Hebrew for "the Lord is peace"
3. **Baal** (ba **all**, or **bale**): a pagan god in Canaan, Hebrew
4. **fleece**: the wooly covering from shearing a sheep
5. **bramble**: thorny bush, obviously not valuable to a farmer
6. **parable**: story or tale containing an important truth or moral lesson (from Latin *parabola*, "comparison")

COMPREHENSION QUESTIONS

1. What message did the angel give Gideon? "The Lord is with you, you mighty man of valor." (p. 192)

2. What signs did God give Gideon to prove he was being called? The first night, He wet a fleece with dew and left the ground dry; the next night, He did the opposite. (pp. 193-194)

3. Why did God prevent Gideon from taking all his willing servants to battle with him? God wanted to prevent the Israelites from thinking they had defeated the Midianites on their own, without God's help. (p. 194)

4. What test did Gideon use to decrease his army to only 300 men? He selected only those who drank at the water by lapping like a dog. (p. 194)

5. What battle cry did the Israelites shout at the camp of Midianites? The Israelites shouted, "The sword of the Lord and of Gideon!" (p. 196)

6. How did Gideon's small army defeat the Midianites? The Midianites were frightened and confused by the shouts, trumpets, breaking pitchers, and lights of Gideon's men. (p. 196)

7. Narrate the parable of the bramble. Who is the bramble? Why? Find the parable on pp. 198-199. Trees are tall and majestic, but the bramble is lowly and despised. Abimelech was a leader without honor.

GEOGRAPHY

1. Locate on your map and memorize:
   - ☐ Midian
   - ☐ Mt. Gerizim
   - ☐ Shechem
   - ☐ Jezreel

BIG PICTURE OF THE BIBLE

- **Judges 2:11, 3:7; 12, 4:1**, and **10:6:** What phrase is repeated in these verses?
- **Judges 2:18:** What does this verse reveal about how the Lord felt towards His people in the midst of their failures during the period of the Judges?
- **Isaiah 9:4:** Who is the "You" being likened to Gideon in this verse?
- **Hebrews 11:32-34:** What do these verses tell us about the Judges?

MEMORY WORK

Use a chalk or dry-erase board to help the students continue to memorize the first five books of the Bible, or Pentateuch.

1. Genesis
2. Exodus
3. Leviticus
4. Numbers
5. Deuteronomy

GEOGRAPHY

Gideon and Midianites:

- Ophrah is 6 miles SW of **Shechem**.
- Mt. Gilead, the Well of Harod, and Hill of Moreh lie in the valley of **Jezreel**.

Jotham and Abimelech:

- Lebanon lies beyond the northern border of Israel.
- Thebez lies about 7 miles NW of **Shechem**.

ACTIVITIES

- pp. 192-193: Identify the two men in the picture.
  An angel of the Lord visits with Gideon as he threshes the wheat.

- pp. 194-195: What are the men doing? Who is watching, and what is he looking for?
  The men are getting water, and Gideon is looking for those who lap the water with their tongues like dogs. They will be his army.

- pp. 196-197: Who is at war in the picture? Who is Gideon?
  Gideon leads his mighty men in war with the Midianites.

- pp. 198-199: Find Abimelech in the picture. Who has killed him?
  A woman dropped a millstone over the wall and killed Abimelech with it.

LESSON 4

BACKGROUND AND SUMMARY

Though the Lord was consistently faithful to his delinquent people, the story of the Judges offers more tragedy than triumph. We see Judges, such as Jephthah and Samson, with such promise and potential for leading the people, reduced to miserably tragic heroes. Not only did the Judges fail, but the people turned from fighting their enemies to fighting each other (Judges 20-21). With the nation struck by civil war, the book of Judges concludes with a final statement of utter hopelessness and confusion: Judges 21:25.

The story of this lesson is as follows:

- Jephthah agrees to fight against the Ammonites; he makes a vow to offer the first thing out of his door upon his return from victory.
- He battles and is victorious.
- His daughter comes out of the door.
- He rends his clothes, but she agrees the vow cannot be broken.
- She goes to her maids and mourns.
- Jephthah offers her to the Lord.
- Israel enslaved 40 years by Philistia.
- Samson dedicated to the Lord.
- He kills a lion and gets honey from its carcass.
- At his marriage feast, his riddle is given away by his wife and he takes revenge on 30 Philistines.
- He sets 300 foxes on Philistine fields.
- He slays 1,000 men with a jawbone.
- He was a judge over Israel 20 years.
- Samson tells his secret and Delilah cuts his hair; he is captured.
- He causes the house of Dagon to collapse, and all inside die.

LESSON 4: Jephthah's Vow | Samson and the Philistines
Golden Children's Bible: pp. 200-209 (Judges 11, 13-16)

FACTS TO KNOW

1. **Jephthah**: defeated Ammonites; sacrificed his daughter
2. **Ammonites**: enemies of Israel that lived across the Jordan River
3. **Samson**: strongest man in the Bible
4. **Philistines**: enemies of Israel; lived on the seacoast of Canaan near Gaza
5. **Delilah**: Samson's Philistine wife
6. **Dagon**: false god of the Philistines
7. **vow**: a solemn promise or special commitment

MEMORY VERSE

> **JUDGES 21:25**
>
> *In those days there was no king in Israel: every man did that which was right in his own eyes.*

1. What does it mean that "every man did that which was right in his own eyes"?
   The people neglected God's ways and did as they saw fit.

2. Who has led the people instead of a king?
   The Judges have led Israel.

3. What has been the Israelites' pattern throughout the period of the Judges?
   The people turned away from God, God allowed their enemies to take control, the people cried out to God for help, and God sends a judge to deliver them.

4. This is the last verse of the book of Judges and it anticipates a change in Israel. Who will rise to lead the people next?
   Israel will soon have a king: Saul, a king of the peoples' choosing, then David, God's choice of king.

VOCABULARY AND EXPRESSIONS

1. **vow**: solemn promise or special commitment
2. **bewailed**: expressed deep, intense sorrow and sadness
3. **"no razor shall come near his head, for he is dedicated to God from birth"**: also known as the "Nazirite vow," meaning separated or dedicated, which held strict regulations on diet and appearance for these men that were set apart for a particular service to God. Others dedicated to God by the Nazirite vow included the prophet Samuel and John the Baptist.
4. **shocks**: piles of sheaves of grain or stalks of corn set up in a field for drying

COMPREHENSION QUESTIONS

1. What rash vow did Jephthah make with God? ___Jephthah pledged that if God allowed him to defeat the Ammonites, he would sacrifice the first thing that came out of the door. (p. 200)___

2. What was the sad consequence of his bargain? ___Jephthah was obliged to sacrifice his only daughter. (pp. 200-201)___

3. What message did an angel give Samson's mother? ___After her barrenness, an angel announced she would have a son dedicated to God; to drink no wine nor eat unclean food nor ever shave his hair. (p. 202)___

4. List some ways Samson displayed his physical strength. ___Samson killed a lion with his bare hands, killed the 30 men of Ashkelon, broke free of ropes with which he had been tied, killed 1,000 men with a donkey's jawbone, and brought down the Philistine house. (pp. 203-209)___

5. Complete Samson's riddle: "Out of the eater came forth ___meat___, and out of the strong came forth ___sweetness___." How did his riddle start a war? ___The conflict began when the Philistines forced the answer from Samson's wife and aroused Samson's great anger. (pp. 202-203)___

6. How did Delilah betray Samson? ___Delilah revealed to the Philistines how to rob Samson of his strength. (pp. 206-207)___

GEOGRAPHY

1. Locate on your map and memorize:
   - ☐ Philistia
   - ☐ Gaza
   - ☐ Ashkelon
   - ☐ Ammon

Lesson 4: Jephthah's Vow | Samson and the Philistines   **15**

BIG PICTURE OF THE BIBLE

- **Deuteronomy 17:14-20:** What are the expectations of Israel's king given in the law of Moses? Who does this passage ultimately describe?
- **Amos 2:11-12:** What are God's reasons for sending judgment on Israel and Judah?

MEMORY WORK

Use a chalk or dry-erase board to help the students continue to memorize the first five books of the Bible, or Pentateuch.

1. Genesis
2. Exodus
3. Leviticus
4. Numbers
5. Deuteronomy

GEOGRAPHY

Jephthah's Vow:

- Tob likely lies SE of the Sea of Galilee.
- Aroer was a town in **Moab**.
- Minnith was east of the Jordan.
- Mizpah lies in Gilead.
- Gilead is a mountainous region east of the **Jordan**; **Nebo** is in it.

Samson and the Philistines:

- Timnath lies in **Philistia**.
- **Ashkelon** is a seaport in **Philistia**.
- Lehi is a hill area in SW Israel.
- **Gaza** is a seaport SW of **Ashkelon**.

ACTIVITIES

- pp. 200-201: Identify Jephthah. Explain the look on his face.
  Jephthah is both startled and saddened that his daughter was the first to appear from his door.

- p. 203: What is Samson doing?
  Samson is wrestling a lion.

- pp. 204-205: Who is Samson fighting? What is he holding? How many men did he defeat?
  Samson is fighting the Philistines with the jawbone of a donkey. He killed 1,000 men.

- pp. 206-207: Identify Samson, Delilah. What is happening to Samson? What is being given to Delilah?
  Samson is getting a haircut while Deliah is being paid more than eleven hundred pieces of silver.

- pp. 208-209: Where is Samson? What has happened to his eyes? What is he doing?
  Samson is in the house of the Philistines. Though he had lost his eyes, God gave him enough strength to pull down the pillars of the house.

LESSON 5

BACKGROUND AND SUMMARY

In the midst of all the chaos and unrest plaguing Israel during the period of the Judges, we find in the book of Ruth a picture of friendship and faithfulness. Here we can observe two important truths.

First, God has a desire for all peoples to come to know Him. Though a Moabite, Ruth models how non-Jewish people would come into relationship with God. Through her love and commitment to her mother-in-law, Ruth forsook the pagan gods of her people to worship the true and living God of Israel. Her faith was rewarded by the Lord; a Moabite girl became David's great-grandmother!

Second, Naomi and Ruth had a grave concern in their lives about the men they had lost. The gravity of their concern, and that of all women in the Ancient Near East, stemmed from the fear of loneliness and life without family. Fortunately, there existed in Israel a means of relief for desperate widows called the "kinsman redeemer." When a widow lost her husband, a willing and able male relative would take that widow as his wife in order to care for her and provide her with family. Thus, Boaz displays how a man could redeem his widowed relative from a life of misfortune, poverty, and sorrow.

The story of this lesson is as follows:

- A famine occured in Israel.
- Elimelech takes his family to Moab.
- The women are widowed.
- They go back to Judah because the Lord has blessed the land.
- Orpah leaves, but Ruth binds herself to Naomi, Israel, and God.
- They come to Bethlehem at the beginning of barley harvest.
- Ruth gleans after the reapers in Boaz's fields, Elimelech's kinsman.
- Boaz notices Ruth and shows her kindness, letting her glean much.
- Naomi instructs Ruth to go to Boaz.
- Boaz must offer another kinsman the role of redeemer; he refuses it and Boaz buys the land of the women's husbands, and he takes Ruth as his wife; she bears Obed.

LESSON 5: Ruth

Golden Children's Bible: pp. 210-215 (Ruth 1-4)

FACTS TO KNOW

1. **Ruth**: faithful daughter-in-law
2. **Naomi**: wife of Elimelech; mother-in-law to Ruth
3. **Boaz**: dedicated kinsman of Naomi
4. **kinsman**: relative, family member
5. **glean**: method of collecting wheat by picking up, grain by grain, what is left behind by reapers; to gather bit by bit

MEMORY VERSE

> **RUTH 1:16**
>
> *And Ruth said, Entreat me not to leave thee, or to return from following after thee; for whither thou goest, I will go, and where thou lodgest I will lodge: thy people shall be my people, and thy God, my God.*

1. Whom is Ruth addressing?
   Naomi

2. What character traits does Ruth show here?
   Ruth is showing her love, loyalty, and friendship for Naomi.

3. What does "whither thou goest" mean?
   It means "to where you go."

4. What does Ruth promise Naomi when she says, "Thy people shall be my people, and thy God, my God"?
   Ruth promises to make Israel her people and the Lord her God.

VOCABULARY AND EXPRESSIONS

1. **"glean ears of grain after whoever gives me his permission to do so"**: The privilege of gleaning wheat from the reapers was common for the poor or for foreigners that had no food.

2. **"kinsman redeemer"**: the system that provided familial support for widows, relatives sold into slavery, etc. A kinsman redeemer would take in a relative widow, repurchase land a poor relative had sold outside of the family, or avenge the wrongful death of a relative.

3. **whither**: to where, wherever

COMPREHENSION QUESTIONS

1. Name Naomi's two sons and her two daughters-in-law. Naomi's two sons were Mahlon and Chilion. Naomi's daughters-in-law were Orpah and Ruth. (p. 210)

2. What sacrifices did Ruth make to stay with Naomi? Ruth suffered famine and was separated from her people and homeland. (p. 211)

3. Why did Boaz help Ruth? Boaz had heard of Ruth's sacrifices for and faithfulness to her mother-in-law. (p. 212)

4. Why did Naomi's nearest kinsman refuse to buy the land? He feared risking his own inheritance. (pp. 214-215)

5. How did the Lord bless Ruth, Boaz, and Naomi? The Lord honored Boaz and Ruth with the birth of a son, who was as dear to Naomi as her own son. (p. 215)

6. Who was the son of Ruth and Boaz? What was his significance in Israel? Their son was Obed, father of Jesse. Jesse was the father of David. (p. 215)

GEOGRAPHY

1. Locate on your map and memorize:
   - ☐ Moab
   - ☐ Bethlehem

BIG PICTURE OF THE BIBLE

- **Leviticus 19:9-10** and **Deuteronomy 24:19:** What do these portions of the law of Moses allow misfortunate people to do?
- **Ruth 4:14-15:** Why are the women praising Naomi in this passage?
- **Matthew 1:5:** Who is included in Jesus' genealogy in this verse?

MEMORY WORK

Use a chalk or dry-erase board to help the students continue to memorize the first five books of the Bible, or Pentateuch.

1. Genesis
2. Exodus
3. Leviticus
4. Numbers
5. Deuteronomy

GEOGRAPHY

Ruth:

- **Moab** is SE of Israel, on the east side of the Dead Sea.
- Naomi and Ruth travel from **Moab** to live in **Bethlehem**, which is SW of **Jericho**.

ACTIVITIES

- pp. 210-211: What is Ruth doing in the picture? Describe this kind of work. What is Boaz doing? What did Boaz tell his reapers to do to help Ruth?

  Ruth is gathering the wheat left behind by the reapers while Boaz is watching. This is the work of a poor person. Boaz told his reapers to let Ruth reap even among the sheaves and to let fall some handfuls on purpose for her.

- pp. 212-213: Identify the man and woman under the shade tree. What is he giving her?
  Boaz is offering Ruth grain to eat.

- p. 215: Identify Boaz and Naomi's kinsman. What is the kinsman doing?
  The kinsman has taken off his shoe and offered it to Boaz as a sign that he has given his rights to Naomi's land over to Boaz.

REVIEW LESSON: Unit 1

INSTRUCTIONS

Use the Review Lesson to support mastery of the material presented in the previous five lessons. Drill the Facts to Know orally or have a Facts to Know bee. Students may also write a description next to each fact on a separate piece of paper. Places to Know should be identified on the map at the end of this lesson. Students may work independently or with the teacher to complete the exercises. A test for this unit is included in the back of this book.

SALVATION HISTORY

Conquest of Canaan
The Spies Hide in Jericho
Crossing the Jordan
The Fall of Jericho
The Sun in Gibeon

Period of the Judges
The Prophetess Defeats Sisera
Israel Defeats the Midianites
The Murdering Brother
A Tragic Vow
A Secret Betrayed
The Kinsman Redeemer

People to Know
Joshua
Rahab
Jabin
Sisera
Deborah
Barak
Gideon
Jotham
Abimelech
Jephthah
Samson
Delilah
Ruth
Naomi
Boaz
Obed
Philistines

Places to Know
Jordan River
Ai
Ashkelon
Kedesh
Shechem
Philistia
Bethlehem
Jericho
Gaza
Gibeon
Ajalon
Jezreel
Moab
Mt. Gerizim
Mt. Nebo
Ammon
Midian

Words to Know/Vocabulary
flax: plant cultivated for fiber and oil
spoils: goods and riches taken in war
hewers of wood, drawers of water: bondsmen, slaves
avenge: to inflict punishment in return for harm done
Baal: false god of the Canaanites
Yahweh-Shalom: altar in Ophrah; means "the Lord is peace"
bramble: thorny bush
vow: solemn promise or commitment
Dagon: false god of the Philistines
kinsman: relative, family member
glean: to pick up grain left behind by reapers

Give the corresponding word or phrase:

1. He followed Moses as leader of the Israelites. _____ Joshua
2. This wicked judge killed 70 of his brothers, save Jotham. _____ Abimelech
3. She was a faithful daughter-in-law to Naomi. _____ Ruth
4. where the sun stood still _____ Gibeon
5. These enemies of Israel lived on the seacoast of Canaan. _____ Philistines
6. He defeated the Midianites with 300 men. _____ Gideon
7. the river Israel crossed to enter the Promised Land _____ Jordan
8. She was Ruth's mother-in-law. _____ Naomi
9. He made a rash vow and sacrificed his own daughter. _____ Jephthah
10. He was the strongest man in the Bible. _____ Samson
11. four other names for Canaan _____ Promised Land, Israel, Palestine, Holy Land
12. Gideon's good son that told the parable of the bramble _____ Jotham
13. Samson killed 1,000 Philistines with _____ the jawbone of a donkey
14. She hid spies in Jericho. _____ Rahab the harlot
15. He was Ruth's kinsman redeemer. _____ Boaz
16. They ruled Israel between Joshua and the kings. _____ the Judges
17. She was a judge and prophesied the defeat of Sisera. _____ Deborah
18. two books of the Bible named for women _____ Ruth and Esther
19. the four major judges _____ Deborah, Gideon, Jephthah, Samson
20. She betrayed Samson to the Philistines. _____ Delilah

Match up the Words to Know:

G	1. Yahweh-Shalom	A.	false god of the Philistines
F	2. kinsman	B.	bondsmen, slaves
K	3. glean	C.	goods and riches taken in war
E	4. flax	D.	solemn promise or commitment
J	5. Baal	E.	plant cultivated for fiber and oil
I	6. bramble	F.	relative, family member
H	7. avenge	G.	"the Lord is peace"
C	8. spoils	H.	to inflict punishment for harm done
B	9. hewers of wood, drawers of water	I.	thorny bush
D	10. vow	J.	false god of the Canaanites
A	11. Dagon	K.	to pick up grain left behind by reapers

Review Lesson: Unit 1 (Lessons 1-5)   19

OLD TESTAMENT DRILL QUESTIONS

The drill questions from Christian Studies I have been compiled in the Appendix. These questions will be used in each of the subsequent study guides for Christian Studies. Continue reviewing these as the year progresses.

REVIEW LESSON: Unit 1

TIMELINE REVIEW

Review the Big Picture of the Bible, so students understand the major periods (i.e., Creation, Patriarchs, Exodus, etc.). When they understand the periods, begin filling in the Full Timeline in the Appendix and populate each period with the important people. In this way, they will associate each person with the right events. (Example: Moses = Exodus)

SALVATION HISTORY TIMELINE
Put these events in the correct order.

Conquest of Canaan

3	The Fall of Jericho
4	The Sun in Gibeon
2	Crossing the Jordan
1	The Spies Hide in Jericho

Period of the Judges

6	Israel Defeats the Midianites
5	The Prophetess Defeats Sisera
9	A Secret Betrayed
8	A Tragic Vow
10	The Kinsman Redeemer
7	The Murdering Brother

COMPREHENSION QUESTIONS

1. What was the arrangement Rahab made with the spies? How did she mark her father's house? Rahab promised not to tell the king about the spies if they would save her family. (p. 179) She tied a piece of scarlet cord in the window. (p. 181)

2. How did God assist Joshua in the battles with the Amorites? God stopped the sun and moon so that Joshua's forces could finish the fighting. (p. 188)

3. Why did God prevent Gideon from taking all his willing servants to battle with him? God wanted to prevent the Israelites from thinking they had defeated the Midianites on their own, without God's help. (p. 194)

4. How did Delilah betray Samson? Delilah revealed to the Philistines how to rob Samson of his strength. (pp. 206-207)

5. Who was the son of Ruth and Boaz? What was his significance in Israel? Their son was Obed, father of Jesse. Jesse was the father of David. (p. 215)

20   Review Lesson: Unit 1 (Lessons 1-5)

SCRIPTURE MEMORIZATION

Check each box if you can recite the Scripture verse from memory. Write each from memory or teacher dictation. Be accurate.

☐ Joshua 1:9 _____ Have not I commanded thee? Be strong and of a good courage; be not afraid, neither be thou dismayed: for the Lord thy God is with thee whithersoever thou goest.

☐ Joshua 10:12 _____ Sun, stand thou still upon Gibeon and thou, Moon, in the valley of Ajalon.

☐ Judges 6:1 _____ And the children of Israel did evil in the sight of the Lord: and the Lord delivered them into the hand of Midian seven years.

☐ Judges 21:25 _____ In those days there was no king in Israel: every man did that which was right in his own eyes.

☐ Ruth 1:16 _____ And Ruth said, Entreat me not to leave thee, or to return from following after thee; for whither thou goest, I will go, and where thou lodgest I will lodge: thy people shall be my people, and thy God, my God.

MEMORY VERSES

To recite memory verses, give the first few words and let students complete the verse orally. Students should write the verse from memory or copy it from the lesson.

REVIEW LESSON: Unit 1

MAP WORK

Places to Know

☐ Ai
☐ Ajalon
☐ Ammon
☐ Ashkelon
☐ Bethlehem
☐ Gaza
☐ Gibeon
☐ Jericho
☐ Jezreel

☐ Jordan River
☐ Kedesh
☐ Midian
☐ Moab
☐ Mt. Gerizim
☐ Mt. Nebo
☐ Philistia
☐ Shechem

We recommend that the student first locate and highlight the place to know on the labeled map, then find it and add place names to the blank map during a geography test or drill.

UNIT 1 MAP A

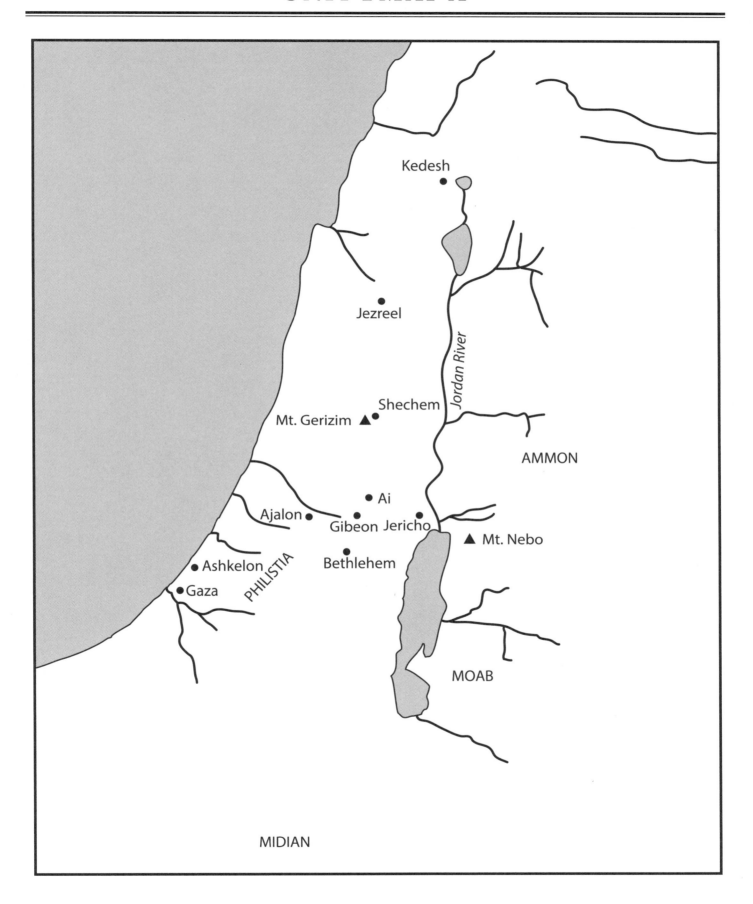

Kedesh

Jezreel

Jordan River

Shechem

Mt. Gerizim ▲

AMMON

Ai

Ajalon

Gibeon Jericho

Mt. Nebo ▲

Bethlehem

Ashkelon

PHILISTIA

Gaza

MOAB

MIDIAN

UNIT 1 MAP B

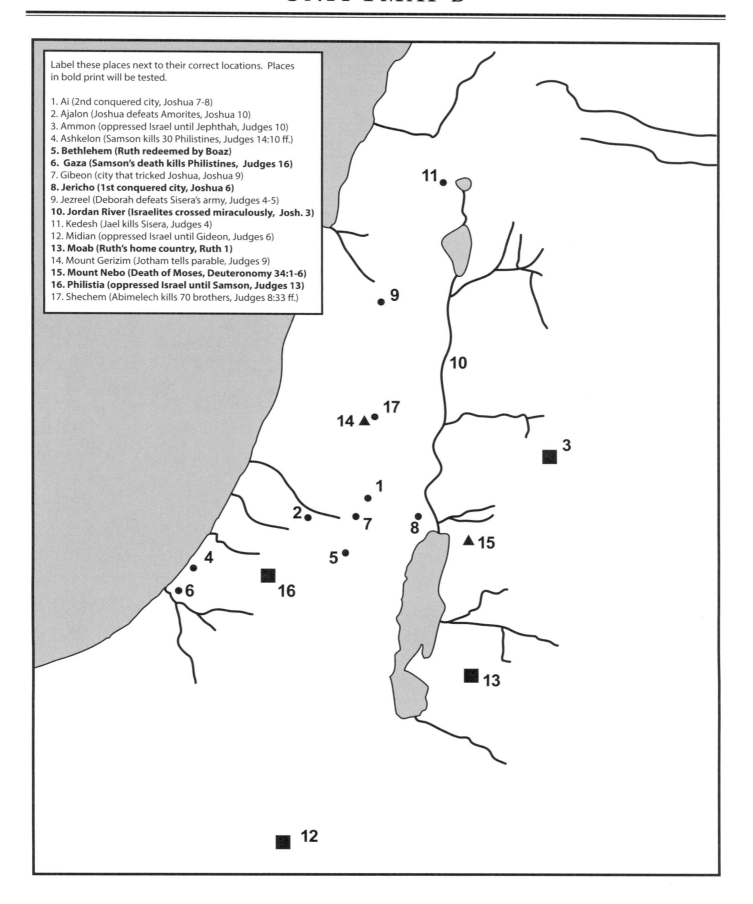

Label these places next to their correct locations. Places in bold print will be tested.

1. Ai (2nd conquered city, Joshua 7-8)
2. Ajalon (Joshua defeats Amorites, Joshua 10)
3. Ammon (oppressed Israel until Jephthah, Judges 10)
4. Ashkelon (Samson kills 30 Philistines, Judges 14:10 ff.)
5. **Bethlehem (Ruth redeemed by Boaz)**
6. **Gaza (Samson's death kills Philistines, Judges 16)**
7. Gibeon (city that tricked Joshua, Joshua 9)
8. **Jericho (1st conquered city, Joshua 6)**
9. Jezreel (Deborah defeats Sisera's army, Judges 4-5)
10. **Jordan River (Israelites crossed miraculously, Josh. 3)**
11. Kedesh (Jael kills Sisera, Judges 4)
12. Midian (oppressed Israel until Gideon, Judges 6)
13. **Moab (Ruth's home country, Ruth 1)**
14. Mount Gerizim (Jotham tells parable, Judges 9)
15. **Mount Nebo (Death of Moses, Deuteronomy 34:1-6)**
16. **Philistia (oppressed Israel until Samson, Judges 13)**
17. Shechem (Abimelech kills 70 brothers, Judges 8:33 ff.)

LESSON 6

BACKGROUND AND SUMMARY

Samuel represents the transition from the period of the Judges to the age of Kings in Israel. He was the last Judge in Israel and anointed Saul, the first king in Israel. As the chief prophet of the Lord, Samuel spoke for God in a time of great change.

Israel had sinned greatly in the eyes of God. The high priest of Israel, Eli, allowed his sons to defame the priesthood through their corruption and take the Ark of the Covenant into battle against the Philistines. For this, the Lord let the Philistines win. The Ark was captured, Eli's sons died in battle, and when he heard the horrible news, Eli fell and broke his neck. But the Lord was making Samuel into a great leader (I Samuel 7:15-17).

When Samuel grew old, the people of Israel requested that he appoint a king over them. Despite Samuel's warnings, they wanted a king like all the other nations (I Sam. 8:5-6,19-20). Thus, the Lord decided to give them exactly what they wanted. Samuel anointed Saul the first king of Israel, for Saul was handsome, tall, and looked like a king. He was the peoples' choice, but Israel would soon learn that image is not everything.

The story of this lesson is as follows:

- Hannah prays for a child, and God gives her Samuel. She dedicates him to serve in the sanctuary of the Lord.
- God calls him and reveals Eli's fall.
- The Philistines capture the Ark.
- Israel asks Samuel for a king.
- God brings Saul to Samuel.
- Saul becomes king, but he disobeys.

VOCABULARY AND EXPRESSIONS

1. **"grew in favor with the Lord and with men"**: Samuel was in good standing with God and those who knew him; said of Jesus in Luke 2:52.

2. **"quit yourselves like men and fight"**: In this sense "quit" means "conduct" or "behave," from *acquit*.

LESSON 6: Samuel and Saul
Golden Children's Bible: pp. 216-224 (I Samuel 1-13)

FACTS TO KNOW

1. **Hannah**: barren mother who gave birth to and dedicated Samuel to the Lord
2. **Samuel**: prophet of God; judged Israel; appointed Saul
3. **Eli**: unfaithful priest at Shiloh who raised Samuel
4. **Shiloh**: house of the Lord where the Ark of the Covenant was kept
5. **Saul**: anointed King of Israel after the people pleaded; a king like the nations had
6. **"Dan to Beersheba"**: from the northernmost city to the southernmost city

MEMORY VERSE

> **I SAMUEL 3:19-20**
>
> *And Samuel grew, and the Lord was with him, and let none of his words fall to the ground. And all Israel from Dan even to Beersheba knew that Samuel was established to be a prophet of the Lord.*

1. What does it mean that the Lord "let none of his words fall to the ground"?
   The Lord made the words of Samuel powerful and important to the people. His words did not go unheard.

2. What does it mean to be "a prophet of the Lord"?
   A prophet speaks for God and tells the people God's will.

3. What does "from Dan to Beersheba" mean? Find these cities on your map and memorize them.
   Dan is far to the north and Beersheba is far to the south. We might say "from Maine to Florida." All of Israel came to respect Samuel as God's prophet.

TEACHER NOTE (SEE ACTIVITIES)

Comparison of Hannah's Song and the Magnificat

- Both Hannah and Mary exalt the Lord for considering their low estate with care.
- Both magnify the holiness and infinite strength of the Lord.
- Both describe the ways in which God supplies the needy and humbles the proud.
- Both list the manifestations of the Lord's might and power.
- Both recall the Lord's faithfulness to Israel.

1. Why did Hannah allow her son to be raised by Eli? <u>Hannah promised the Lord that if He would give her a son, she would then give the child to God's service. (p. 216)</u>

2. What warning did God give Samuel when He spoke to him in the temple? <u>God warned Samuel that he was about to punish Eli for allowing his sons to be wicked priests. (pp. 217-219)</u>

3. What did the elders request of Samuel in his old age? <u>They wanted a king "like all the other nations had." (p. 220)</u>

4. Describe the king that would reign if the people refused to obey Samuel. <u>The king would make Israel a factory for his wars. He will make servants and warriors of their children, take their best lands and take a tenth of their harvest, etc., to sustain his army. (p. 220)</u>

5. From what tribe was Saul? From what family was he? Who was his father? <u>Saul was from the tribe of Benjamin, family of Matri, and son of Kish. (p. 224)</u>

6. What warning did Samuel give Saul? <u>Samuel prophesied, "Your kingdom will not last because you have not kept the commandments of God." (p. 224)</u>

GEOGRAPHY

1. Locate on your map and memorize:
   - ☐ Shiloh
   - ☐ Beersheba
   - ☐ Dan
   - ☐ Philistia

BIG PICTURE OF THE BIBLE

- **I Samuel 1:** What does Hannah feel about her barrenness and God's answer to her prayer?
- **I Samuel 5:1-5:** How did the god of the Philistines bow before the Ark of God in Ashdod?

MEMORY WORK

Use a chalk or dry-erase board to help the students continue to memorize the first five books of the Bible, and start learning the twelve books of History.

1. Joshua
2. Judges
3. Ruth
4. I Samuel
5. II Samuel
6. I Kings
7. II Kings
8. I Chronicles
9. II Chronicles
10. Ezra
11. Nehemiah
12. Esther

GEOGRAPHY

Samuel and Saul:

- **Shiloh** is south of **Shechem** and west of the **Jordan**.
- **Dan** is the northernmost city of Israel, and **Beersheba** is the southernmost.

ACTIVITIES

- pp. 216-217: Identify each person in the picture. Describe the event.
  Samuel's parents are presenting him to Eli for God's service.

- pp. 218-219: What is Samuel doing while Eli sleeps?
  Samuel is listening to God speak.

- p. 221: To whom are these men pleading? What are they asking of him?
  The elders of Israel are asking Samuel for a king like the other nations.

- pp. 222-223: Identify the men in this picture. How can you tell them apart?
  Saul is young, handsome, and tall. Saul is older and shorter.

- pp. 224-225: What is happening in the picture?
  Samuel is anointing Saul as king of Israel by pouring oil on his head.

- Read Hannah's Song (I Samuel 2:1-10) and the Magnificat (Luke 1:46-55, p. 349). How are they similar? (See Teacher Note on p. 26.)

LESSON 7

BACKGROUND AND SUMMARY

Everything seemed to be going well. Saul was winning victories over the enemies of Israel and strengthening the army. His appearance, however, was deceiving. After Saul impatiently offered sacrifices in place of the priest, Samuel prophesied that the Lord would take away the kingdom from him. The downward spiral of Saul's career ended in his disobedience with the spoils of the Amalekites. From Saul's grave mistakes we can glean two important lessons.

First, God desires simple obedience to His word more than our best intended sacrifices. In his choice to keep back the spoils of the Amalekites, Saul revealed that his heart feared people more than God. Thus, Saul had totally reversed the expectations of Israel's king as given by Moses. For his punishment, the Lord would rip the kingdom from him.

Second, the judgments of man cannot compare to the wisdom of God. The people desired a king like the nations (i.e., Saul). But such was not the king Israel needed. The Lord knew David's heart and judged he would be a good king. Will we lean on our own understanding rather than God's timeless wisdom, as Israel did? Let us not forsake the wisdom of God in the decisions we must make (Proverbs 3:5-7).

The story of this lesson is as follows:
- The people ask Samuel for a king.
- Saul, searching for asses from Mt. Ephraim, meets Samuel. Saul is anointed king, but tells no one.
- Saul is proclaimed king at Mizpeh, but he hides among the baggage.
- Jonathan unintentionally breaks his father's foolish oath. Before Saul can kill him, the people intervene.
- Saul is told to utterly destroy Amalek, but he spares the best of the spoils.
- Samuel says God will take the kingdom away from Saul and give it to a better man.
- God sends Samuel to anoint David.
- David is sent to play the harp for Saul, to soothe his mind.

LESSON 7: Jonathan Breaks the Oath | David
Golden Children's Bible: pp. 225-229 (I Samuel 14-16)

FACTS TO KNOW
1. **Jonathan**: son of Saul, David's best friend
2. **David**: son of Jesse, anointed king by Samuel
3. **anointed**: act of being ceremonially chosen by God
4. **Amalekites**: descendants of Amalek, king who threatened Israel during the Exodus

MEMORY VERSE

> **I SAMUEL 16:7**
>
> *For the Lord seeth not as man seeth; for man looketh on the outward appearance, but the Lord looketh on the heart.*

1. Why was David the last son to be presented as a potential king?
   David was the youngest and an unlikely choice of king, so he was out tending his father's sheep.

2. Explain "man looketh on the outward appearance."
   People only see what is on the surface and often do not make valid assessments because they are distracted by superficial exteriors.

3. Why does God judge the goodness of a man by his heart? What can be found there?
   God does not care about outward appearances, only the true character of a person, which is found in the heart.

VOCABULARY AND EXPRESSIONS

1. **oath**: promise or vow
2. **"lots were chosen"**: also known as "casting lots," a process where names are drawn or determined by an arbitrary test, similar to rolling the dice. This practice reveals the basic Old Testament belief that God was in complete control of everything; therefore, He would reveal the desired answer through this simple process.
3. **"I regret that I have set up Saul to be king."**: When we apply the human language of regret or remorse to the Lord, we must remember that God is all-knowing and unchanging and that sometimes our best language cannot fully describe His thoughts or emotions. Phrases like this should be balanced with what Samuel says on the next page about God's constancy (p. 227 or I Samuel 15:29).

1. What were God's instructions to Saul? How did Saul disobey Him? _____ God commanded Saul to destroy the Amalekites and their possessions completely. Saul disobeyed by keeping the best of the spoils. (p. 226)

2. What was Saul's excuse for his disobedience? _____ Saul feared the people and gave in to their demands. (p. 227)

3. What were the consequences of Saul's decision? _____ The Lord rejected him and he lost control of Israel as king. (p. 227)

4. Where did God send Samuel to find the next chosen king? _____ The Lord sent him to Bethlehem to the family of Jesse. (p. 228)

5. Why was David an unlikely choice for Israel's new king? _____ David was the youngest son of Jesse, which gave him less "clout" than his brothers, as birth order was a significant thing at the time. David was a young man and a humble shepherd. (p. 228)

6. How were Saul and David acquainted? _____ Saul asked for a harp player to relieve him of bad spirits with soothing music. Saul's servant sent David, who was an accomplished musician. (pp. 228-229)

GEOGRAPHY

1. Locate on your map and memorize:
   - ☐ Moab
   - ☐ Ramah
   - ☐ Amalek
   - ☐ Ammon

Lesson 7: Jonathan Breaks the Oath | David   29

BIG PICTURE OF THE BIBLE

God is the chief hero of His story. Amid the failures of Saul, we see glimpses of hope from those who recognize the Lord as the great hero of history. When Saul disappoints, consider his son.

- **I Samuel 14:1-23:** How is Jonathan courageous? In verse 6, from where do we see his courage coming?

TEACHER NOTE
"the evil spirit from God came upon Saul"

We must be careful to make clear the fact that God is not the author of evil (James 1:13). Instead, this expression means that even the evil spirits and devils can only trouble Saul if God allows it. At this point, Saul is very vulnerable to psychological and spiritual attacks because of his sin.

MEMORY WORK
Review the twelve books of History.

1.	Joshua	7.	II Kings
2.	Judges	8.	I Chronicles
3.	Ruth	9.	II Chronicles
4.	I Samuel	10.	Ezra
5.	II Samuel	11.	Nehemiah
6.	I Kings	12.	Esther

GEOGRAPHY
Jonathan Breaks the Oath:

- The people of **Amalek** live SW of Israel toward Egypt.
- **Ramah** is Samuel's home.

ACTIVITIES

- p. 226: Identify the animals at the top of the page. Where did they come from?
  These are the choice sheep, cattle, and goats of the Amalekites that should have been destroyed by Saul.

- p. 227: Who are the two men pictured here? What has happened to the older man's red robe? Why?
  Samuel has told Saul that the Lord has torn the kingdom of Israel from Saul just like Saul tore the skirt of Samuel's mantle.

- p. 229: Identify the people in the king's court. Why is David there?
  David is playing his harp for Saul, to soothe his troubled mind.

- Draw a family tree including David, Jesse, Obed, Ruth, Boaz, and Naomi.

LESSON 8

BACKGROUND AND SUMMARY

Not long after David was anointed by Samuel, he began to display the character qualities that set him apart from Saul. In his encounter with Goliath, David's heart for God became visible for all of Israel and even the Philistines.

David made two very significant statements that revealed the nature of his heart for God. First, when David visited Israel's camp and heard Goliath's challenge, he responded with unique revulsion. In I Samuel 17:26, he asked, "Who is this uncircumcised Philistine that he should defy the armies of the living God?" David understood what others missed, namely that Goliath had insulted not Israel but Israel's God.

Second, when David went out to meet Goliath, he faced the great warrior with a singular, resolute confidence. When Goliath teased and taunted the young shepherd boy, David answered him boldly, saying, "Thou comest to me with a sword, and with a spear, and with a shield: but I come to thee in the name of the Lord of hosts. This day will the Lord deliver thee into mine hand; and I will smite thee; that all the earth may know that there is a God in Israel." David's trust rested in the name of the Lord. (Compare David's certainty with Jonathan's hope in I Samuel 14:6.) It was for God's name that David opposed Goliath, not his own glory. David knew in his heart that the Lord would not suffer the blasphemy of Goliath any longer.

In this way, David pictures for us the King of Kings, for we see the same heart in Jesus. In the Garden of Gethsemane, eager for the victory of God over the seed of the serpent, Jesus prayed to his Father, "not as I will, but as thou wilt" (Matthew 26:39).

The story of this lesson is as follows:

- Philistines and Israel meet at Valley of Elah, west of Jerusalem.
- Goliath challenges Israelites; Israel is frightened 40 days.
- David sent to get news for Jesse.
- David offers to fight.
- David defeats Goliath and Israel chases Philistines.
- Saul takes notice of David.

LESSON 8: David and Goliath
Golden Children's Bible: pp. 230-235 (I Samuel 17)

FACTS TO KNOW

1. **Goliath**: giant champion of Philistines; killed by David
2. **Valley of Elah**: site of Israel's camp in the battle against the Philistines
3. **mail**: fabric of linked metal ringlets, worn as armor
4. **shekel**: unit of weight, equal to about half an ounce
5. **Eliab**: David's eldest brother

MEMORY VERSE

> **I SAMUEL 17:45-46**
>
> *Then David said to the Philistine, Thou comest to me with a sword, and with a spear, and with a shield: but I come to thee in the name of the Lord of hosts. ... This day will the Lord deliver thee into mine hand; and I will smite thee ... that all the earth may know that there is a God in Israel.*

1. To whom is David speaking in this verse?
   David is speaking to Goliath, the champion of the Philistines.

2. What does it mean to "deliver thee into mine hand"? To "smite"?
   "Deliver into mine hand" means to be given over in defeat. "Smite" means to kill.

3. Why is David so sure that he can kill the Philistine giant?
   David was completely confident that the Lord would demonstrate His power over the Philistines and make His name great on all the earth.

VOCABULARY AND EXPRESSIONS

1. **"Lord of hosts"**: title for God that expresses His supreme power and might. The term *hosts* could refer to earthly armies, heavenly bodies, or heavenly armies. It is a general statement about God's universal preeminence over all natural and supernatural powers.

2. **"I will give your flesh to the fowls of the air, and to the beasts of the field."**: Goliath's expression means that when he kills David, he will leave his body for the wild animals to scavenge.

3. **stripling**: youth or young man

4. **Bethlehemite**: a person from the town of Bethlehem

COMPREHENSION QUESTIONS

1. Describe Goliath. ___Goliath stood 9 feet, 9 inches tall and wore a helmet of brass, a
coat of mail, and brass shin guards. He carried a brass shield and held an iron spear.
(p. 230)

2. What was the challenge that Goliath taunted Israel with each day? ___Goliath challenged the
Israelite army to one-on-one combat. The winner would enslave the loser. (p. 230)

3. How did David convince Saul that he was an able fighter? ___David told Saul that as a shepherd
he had killed a lion and a bear while protecting his sheep. (p. 233)

4. List the many ways that Goliath had the advantage in his fight with David. What was David's advantage?
Goliath exceeded David in age, size, experience, and weaponry. But the Lord fought
for David, and God is stronger than even the greatest warrior on earth. (pp. 230-233)

5. What was the outcome of their fight? ___David killed Goliath with the stone from his sling
and then cut off his head. The Philistines fled in fear at what Israel's God had done,
but Israel chased and plundered them. (p. 234)

GEOGRAPHY

1. Locate on your map and memorize:
   ☐ Gath

BIG PICTURE OF THE BIBLE

- **Psalm 115:** How does this psalm show the victory of Israel's God?
- **Colossians 1:13-14, 2:13-15:** Why is Christ's victory greater than David's?

MEMORY WORK

Continue to review the Old Testament books (5-12-5-5-12). This week, review the five books of Wisdom.

1. Job
2. Psalms
3. Proverbs
4. Ecclesiastes
5. Song of Solomon

GEOGRAPHY

David and Goliath:

- The Valley of Elah means "the valley of the oak or terebinth." To this day there are terebinth trees in the Valley of Elah. It is almost midway between **Bethlehem** and the sea, near **Gath**.
- **Gath** is Goliath's hometown in **Philistia**.

ACTIVITIES

- p. 231: Who is pictured here? What is he doing in the picture?
  Goliath is taunting the Israelites to come out and fight him one-on-one.

- pp. 232-233: Who is being led through the Israelite camp? Why are the soldiers sitting around instead of preparing to fight?
  David is being led through the camp and is surprised that all of Israel's army is afraid to face the Philistine giant.

- pp. 234-235: Identify those pictured here. Describe the look on little David's face. What is going to happen next?
  David is about to kill Goliath and will soon cut off his head. David's face shows his anger at the way Goliath insulted the God of Israel.

- **Copybook Verse Review:** #27-28 in Appendix.

LESSON 9

BACKGROUND AND SUMMARY

The kingdom of Israel was taken from Saul and given to David. Along with the removal of God's spirit and the onset of demonic frustrations, Saul began to grow very antagonistic toward David. The young hero excelled in warfare and in playing the harp, and for both Saul depended upon him. His dependence on David only added to his rage when coupled with David's budding popularity with the people. Awaiting the proper time to receive that which God had already given him, David took increasingly inventive measures to avoid Saul's wrath. Amidst Saul's psychological and political collapse, however, we find another glorious picture of faithful friendship: David and Jonathan.

The value of examining their friendship lies in the model of selfless love given us in Jonathan. Too often reminded by his father (I Samuel 20:30-32), Jonathan knew well that David's success would mean his loss of a future throne. Rather than reject David, Jonathan preferred to obediently submit to what the Lord was doing with him. In this way, Jonathan is a model for us of selfless love and loyal friendship.

The story of this lesson is as follows:

- After defeating the Philistines, Saul makes David a military leader.
- David becomes popular, and Saul feels threatened.
- Saul tries to kill David in various ways.
- David escapes from Saul with Michal's help and takes refuge with Samuel at Ramah.
- David and Jonathan make a covenant of friendship.
- Saul tries to strike Jonathan for protecting David.
- Jonathan sends David away for his protection.

LESSON 9: Saul's Jealousy | David and Jonathan

Golden Children's Bible: pp. 236-241 (I Samuel 18-20)

FACTS TO KNOW

1. **Merab**: Saul's oldest daughter
2. **Michal**: David's wife; Saul's younger daughter
3. **Abner**: general of Saul's army
4. **tabret**: an instrument like a timbrel or tambourine
5. **javelin**: a small spear

MEMORY VERSE

> **I SAMUEL 18:7**
>
> *And the women answered one another as they played and said, Saul hath slain his thousands, and David his ten thousands.*

1. Why are the women celebrating David in song?
   They were saying that David was a greater warrior than Saul.

2. How does Saul react when he hears the song of the women?
   "And from this time forward Saul eyed David with suspicion." (p. 236)

3. Why does Saul feel threatened?
   Saul feared that because David was popular with the people, he would lose his throne to the giant-slayer.

VOCABULARY AND EXPRESSIONS

1. **dowry**: a gift or offering given to the man when he takes a wife

2. **"covenant of friendship"**: a pledge of mutual loyalty with God as their witness

3. **reckon**: to consider or calculate

4. **"son of a perverse, rebellious woman"**: Saul insults the character of his son as though he were from a wicked mother. The insult is aimed at Jonathan, not his mother.

COMPREHENSION QUESTIONS

1. Why was David credited with slaying "ten thousands" in the women's song? __The women of__ the cities of Israel proclaimed David a hero ten times greater than Saul, because David's victory over Goliath resulted in a triumph over the whole Philistine army. (p. 236)

2. How did Saul conspire to kill David indirectly? ___Saul tried to make David his general,___ hoping that David would die in battle. (p. 236)

3. What did Saul ask of David instead of a dowry for his daughter's hand? __Instead of a dowry, Saul__ required David to kill 100 Philistines in order to marry Michal. (p. 238)

4. How did Saul's children, Jonathan and Michal, help protect David from their father? __Michal helped__ David escape from the palace in the night, and Jonathan warned David about his father's murderous plans after he could not change Saul's mind about David. (p. 239)

5. How did David and Jonathan secretly communicate about Saul's intent? __When Jonathan shot__ 3 arrows and sent a servant to retrieve them, he would alert David to Saul's plans by directing his servant. If the arrows went "beyond" the boy, David was to flee because Saul wanted to kill him. (p. 240)

BIG PICTURE OF THE BIBLE

- **Psalm 35:** David's prayer that God would rescue him for the pursuit of his enemies. How does the imagery of this psalm of David relate to the specific details of the story?

MEMORY WORK

Continue to review the Old Testament books (5-12-5-5-12). This week, review the five books of the Major Prophets.

1. Isaiah
2. Jeremiah
3. Lamentations
4. Ezekiel
5. Daniel

ACTIVITIES

- pp. 236-237: Describe the scene at the top of these pages.
  The women are coming out of the city singing their song of praise for David's victory over Goliath.

- p. 238: What is happening in the picture? Why?
  An evil spirit has seized Saul; he is trying to kill David with a javelin.

- p. 239: Who is climbing down the wall? Why? Who is the woman?
  David is fleeing the palace, because Saul's men have come to kill him. Michal, his wife, is helping David escape.

- p. 240: What is happening in the picture? How are David and Jonathan communicating? What is the message?
  Jonathan is signaling David to beware of Saul by shooting the arrow beyond the servant. David must flee!

- **Copybook Verse Review:** #29 in Appendix.

LESSON 10

BACKGROUND AND SUMMARY

It was clear that the hand of God had completely left Saul and resided upon David. Aside from the inclusion of some important characters in the life of David (Abiathar, high priest in Israel until the time of Solomon, and Abigail, wife of David and mother of Kileab), this section contains two very significant character lessons.

First, the lust for power and the desperation to keep it can lead one to commit unthinkable atrocities. Upon finding that Ahimelech aided David in his escape, Saul issued a heinously homicidal order to his men, demanding the murder of all God's priests. Saul's men were so horrified by his orders that they refused their king! Could the moral descent of the king sink lower than killing the priests of the Lord?

Second, the fear of God should rule over our selfish desires. More than once (I Samuel 24, 26), David had the opportunity to make an end of Saul, but he would not do it. Though David knew the throne would be his in time, he respected the sanctity of the king's office of ministry. David trusted God and was content to await God's plan; that is why he did not kill Saul when he had the chance.

The story of this lesson is as follows:

- Ahimelech the priest helps David.
- David becomes captain of 400 men.
- Saul has Doeg kill the priests.
- Abiathar the priest joins David.
- David goes to the wilderness, and his company protects the men of Nabal. So, David sends to request food from Nabal, but he is denied.
- David sets out to slaughter Nabal and his servants, but Abigail intercepts him and calms his anger.
- Nabal is struck dead by God, and Abigail marries David.
- David sneaks into Saul's camp and steals his spear and water jug. He reveals himself from afar, and Saul apologizes for his sin and foolishness.
- David and Saul go their ways.

FACTS TO KNOW

1. **Ahimelech**: priest of Nob; assisted David; killed by Saul
2. **Doeg the Edomite**: foremost herdsman of Saul; betrayed David and Ahimelech
3. **Abiathar**: son of Ahimelech; told David that Saul had killed the priests
4. **Nabal**: foolish landowner in Carmel
5. **Abigail**: wise woman who became David's wife

MEMORY VERSE

PSALM 121

I will lift up mine eyes unto the hills, from whence cometh my help.
My help cometh from the Lord, which made heaven and earth.

He will not suffer thy foot to be moved: he that keepeth thee will not slumber.
Behold, he that keepeth Israel shall neither slumber nor sleep.

The Lord is thy keeper: the Lord is thy shade upon thy right hand.
The sun shall not smite thee by day nor the moon by night.

The Lord shall preserve thee from all evil: he shall preserve thy soul.

The Lord shall preserve thy going out and thy coming in from this time forth, and even for evermore.

VOCABULARY AND EXPRESSIONS

1. **"the hallowed bread"**: the "bread of the Presence" or "showbread" used in the Tabernacle

2. **churlish**: vulgar or uncivil

3. **"son of Belial"**: A child of the devil was an Old Testament name for the devil.

COMPREHENSION QUESTIONS

1. When David visited the priest at Nob, how did the priest assist him? ___Ahimelech gave David some of the sacred bread and also the sword of Goliath.___

2. How did Saul punish the priests of Nob? Why? ___Saul had the city of Nob destroyed and killed the 85 priests that helped David and withheld his whereabouts. (p. 242)___

3. Who became David's loyal companion? ___Abiathar, the son of Ahimelech, was the only one to survive the destruction of Nob, and he fled to David for refuge. (p. 243)___

4. How did Abigail gain David's admiration and love? ___Abigail rode out to meet David, apologized for her husband's insult, and asked him to remember her in triumph. (p. 245)___

5. What did David take from beside Saul's pillow? Why? ___David took the spear and jug of water from beside Saul's pillow to show the king that he had an opportunity to kill him but did not take it. (p. 246)___

6. How did Saul react to David's humanity in sparing his life? ___Saul blessed David and stopped pursuing him. (p. 246)___

GEOGRAPHY

1. Locate on your map and memorize:
   ☐ Nob
   ☐ Edom
   ☐ Carmel

BIG PICTURE OF THE BIBLE

- **I Samuel 24:1-12:** How was David's first opportunity to kill Saul comical? What was David resolved about?
- **Psalm 30, 31, 57,** and **59:** More psalms of David that contain his prayers to God for salvation from the enemies (e.g., Saul) that have come after him.

MEMORY WORK

Continue to review the Old Testament books (5-12-5-5-12). This week, review the twelve books of the Minor Prophets. There will be a test over all the books in next week's Review Lesson.

1. Hosea	**7.** Nahum
2. Joel	**8.** Habakkuk
3. Amos	**9.** Zephaniah
4. Obadiah	**10.** Haggai
5. Jonah	**11.** Zechariah
6. Micah	**12.** Malachi

GEOGRAPHY

Saul's Wrath:

- **Nob** is in north Israel, near the Sea of Galilee. It is the place of Abiathar the priest.
- Doeg is a man of **Edom**, or the descendants of Esau, who live south of the Dead Sea.

David and Abigail:

- Abigail lived in **Carmel**, a town south of **Bethlehem** towards **Beersheba**.

ACTIVITIES

- pp. 242-243: Describe the scene at the top of these pages. What command is being given?
  Saul is about to punish Ahimelech and the priests of Nob for helping David. Saul is commanding Doeg the Edomite to slay the priests and utterly destroy the city.

- p. 243: Identify the men in the picture at the bottom of the page.
  Ahimelech is giving David the sword of Goliath.

- pp. 244-245: Who is pictured here with David? What is she doing?
  Abigail met David on the way to Carmel to give him food and supplies. She is bowing low before him, asking for his mercy.

- p. 247: Identify the man with the spear. What is he doing? Who is sleeping?
  David has crept into the tent of the king and taken a spear and water jug even as Saul and his men sleep.

REVIEW LESSON: Unit 2

INSTRUCTIONS

Use the Review Lesson to support mastery of the material presented in the previous five lessons. Drill the Facts to Know orally or have a Facts to Know Bee. Students may also write a description next to each fact on a separate piece of paper. Places to Know should be identified on the map at the end of this lesson. Students may work independently or with the teacher to complete the exercises. A test for this unit is included in the back of this book.

SALVATION HISTORY

Reign of Saul
The People's King Anointed
Keeping the Amalekite Spoils
Samuel Anoints God's King
Shepherd Boy Smites a Giant
The King's Wrath

People to Know
Hannah
Samuel
Eli
Saul
Jonathan
David
Goliath
Merab
Michal
Abner
Ahimelech
Doeg the Edomite
Abiathar
Nabal
Abigail

Places to Know
Amalek
Edom
Beersheba
Carmel
Gath
Ramah
Shiloh
Nob
Dan
Bethlehem
Jerusalem

Books of the O. T.
5-12-5-5-12

Genesis
Exodus
Leviticus
Numbers
Deuteronomy

Joshua
Judges
Ruth
I, II Samuel
I, II Kings
I, II Chronicles
Ezra
Nehemiah
Esther

Job
Psalms
Proverbs
Ecclesiastes
Song of Solomon

Isaiah
Jeremiah
Lamentations
Ezekiel
Daniel

Hosea
Joel
Amos
Obadiah
Jonah
Micah
Nahum
Habakkuk
Zephaniah
Haggai
Zechariah
Malachi

Words to Know/Vocabulary
anointed: act of being ceremonially selected or chosen
mail: fabric of linked metal ringlets, worn as armor
shekel: unit of weight, equal to about half an ounce
tabret: an instrument like a timbrel or tambourine
javelin: a small spear
prophet: one who speaks for God, reveals God's will

Give the corresponding word or phrase:

1. This priest of Shiloh had corrupt sons. _____Eli_____

2. She pledged to give her child to the service of the Lord. _____Hannah_____

3. He was the last judge and a great prophet of God. _____Samuel_____

4. He was the people's choice of king for Israel. _____Saul_____

5. The elders of Israel wanted a king like _____"all the other nations"_____

6. God said he was a "man after his own heart." _____David_____

7. He was the son of Kish from the Tribe of Benjamin. _____Saul_____

8. the prayer of Samuel's mother _____Hannah's Song_____

9. He was Saul's son and David's best friend. _____Jonathan_____

10. He was the son of Jesse from the Tribe of Judah. _____David_____

11. where Samuel found the shepherd boy to be king of Israel _____Bethlehem_____

12. the Philistine giant that insulted Israel's God _____Goliath_____

13. David's eldest brother that told him to go home _____Eliab_____

14. This was David's weapon of choice against Goliath. _____a stone and a sling_____

15. David's first wife and the daughter of Saul _____Michal_____

16. David played this to soothe Saul. _____harp_____

17. the general of Saul's army _____Abner_____

18. the wise lady of Carmel that became David's second wife _____Abigail_____

19. the number of times that David spared Saul's life _____twice_____

20. "For the Lord does not see as man sees. Man looks on the _____outward appearance_____,

    but the Lord looks at the _____heart_____."

Match up the Words to Know

F	1. anointed	A.	a small spear
D	2. mail	B.	speaks for God
E	3. shekel	C.	like a tambourine
B	4. prophet	D.	worn as armor
C	5. tabret	E.	about half an ounce
A	6. javelin	F.	ceremonially chosen

OLD TESTAMENT DRILL QUESTIONS

The drill questions from Christian Studies I have been compiled in the Appendix. These questions will be used in each of the subsequent study guides for Christian Studies. Continue reviewing these as the year progresses.

REVIEW LESSON: Unit 2

TIMELINE REVIEW

Review the Big Picture of the Bible, so students understand the major periods (i.e., Creation, Patriarchs, Exodus, etc.). When they understand the periods, continue filling in the Full Timeline in the Appendix and populate each period with the important people. In this way, they will associate each person with the right events. (Example: Moses = Exodus)

SALVATION HISTORY TIMELINE
Put these events in the correct order.

Reign of Saul

3	Samuel Anoints God's King
5	The King's Wrath
2	Keeping the Amalekite Spoils
4	Shepherd Boy Smites a Giant
1	The People's King Anointed

COMPREHENSION QUESTIONS

1. Why did Hannah allow her son to be raised by Eli? Hannah promised the Lord that if He would give her a son, she would then give the child to God's service. (p. 216)

2. Why was David an unlikely choice for Israel's new king? David was the youngest son of Jesse, which gave him less "clout" than his brothers, as birth order was a significant thing at the time. David was a young man and a humble shepherd. (p. 228)

3. List the many ways that Goliath had the advantage in his fight with David. What was David's advantage? Goliath exceeded David in age, size, experience, and weaponry. But the Lord fought for David, and God is stronger than even the greatest warrior on earth. (pp. 230-233)

4. How did Saul's children, Jonathan and Michal, help protect David from their father? Michal helped David escape from the palace in the night, and Jonathan warned David about his father's murderous plans after he could not change Saul's mind about David. (p. 239)

5. How did Saul punish the priests of Nob? Why? Saul had the city of Nob destroyed and killed the 85 priests that helped David and withheld his whereabouts. (p. 242)

SCRIPTURE MEMORIZATION

Check each box if you can recite the Scripture verse from memory. Write each from memory or teacher dictation. Be accurate.

☐ I Samuel 3:19-20 _____ And Samuel grew, and the Lord was with him, and let none of his words fall to the ground. And all Israel from Dan even to Beersheba knew that Samuel was established to be a prophet of the Lord. _____

_____

_____

☐ I Samuel 16:7 _____ For the Lord seeth not as man seeth; for man looketh on the outward appearance, but the Lord looketh on the heart. _____

_____

_____

☐ I Samuel 17:45-46 _____ Then David said to the Philistine, Thou comest to me with a sword, and with a spear, and with a shield: but I come to thee in the name of the Lord of hosts. … This day will the Lord deliver thee into mine hand; and I will smite thee … that all the earth may know that there is a God in Israel. _____

_____

☐ I Samuel 18:7 _____ And the women answered one another as they played and said, Saul hath slain his thousands, and David his ten thousands. _____

_____

_____

☐ Psalm 121 _____ I will lift up mine eyes unto the hills, from whence cometh my help. My help cometh from the Lord, which made heaven and earth. He will not suffer thy foot to be moved: he that keepeth thee will not slumber. Behold, he that keepeth Israel shall neither slumber nor sleep. The Lord is thy keeper: the Lord is thy shade upon thy right hand. The sun shall not smite thee by day nor the moon by night. The Lord shall preserve thee from all evil: he shall preserve thy soul. The Lord shall preserve thy going out and thy coming in from this time forth, and even for evermore. _____

_____

_____

Review Lesson: Unit 2 (Lessons 6-10)   39

MEMORY VERSES

To recite memory verses, give the first few words and let students complete the verse orally. Students should write the verse from memory or copy it from the lesson.

REVIEW LESSON: Unit 2

The Books of the Law

1. Genesis
2. Exodus
3. Leviticus
4. Numbers
5. Deuteronomy

The Books of History

1. Joshua
2. Judges
3. Ruth
4. I Samuel
5. II Samuel
6. I Kings
7. II Kings
8. I Chronicles
9. II Chronicles
10. Ezra
11. Nehemiah
12. Esther

The Books of Wisdom

1. Job
2. Psalms
3. Proverbs
4. Ecclesiastes
5. Song of Solomon

The Books of the Major Prophets

1. Isaiah
2. Jeremiah
3. Lamentations
4. Ezekiel
5. Daniel

The Books of the Minor Prophets

1. Hosea
2. Joel
3. Amos
4. Obadiah
5. Jonah
6. Micah
7. Nahum
8. Habakkuk
9. Zephaniah
10. Haggai
11. Zechariah
12. Malachi

MAP WORK

Places to Know

☐ Amalek
☐ Beersheba
☐ Carmel
☐ Dan
☐ Edom

☐ Gath
☐ Nob
☐ Ramah
☐ Shiloh

We recommend that the student first locate and highlight the place to know on the labeled map, then find it and add place names to the blank map during a geography test or drill.

UNIT 2 MAP A

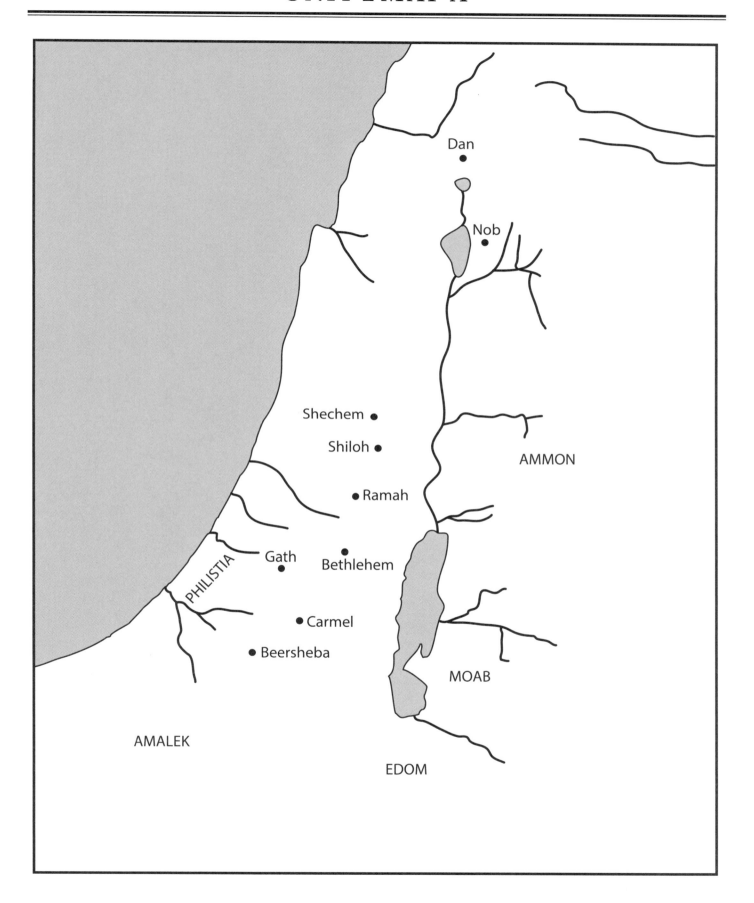

Dan

Nob

Shechem

Shiloh

AMMON

Ramah

Gath

Bethlehem

PHILISTIA

Carmel

Beersheba

MOAB

AMALEK

EDOM

UNIT 2 MAP B

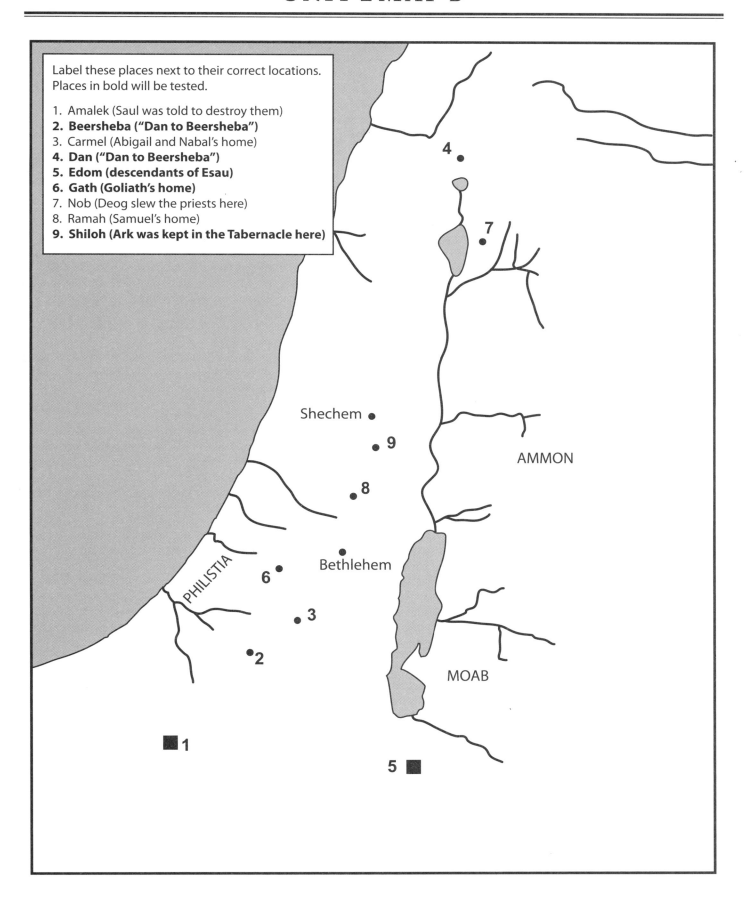

Label these places next to their correct locations. Places in bold will be tested.

1. Amalek (Saul was told to destroy them)
2. **Beersheba ("Dan to Beersheba")**
3. Carmel (Abigail and Nabal's home)
4. **Dan ("Dan to Beersheba")**
5. **Edom (descendants of Esau)**
6. **Gath (Goliath's home)**
7. Nob (Deog slew the priests here)
8. Ramah (Samuel's home)
9. **Shiloh (Ark was kept in the Tabernacle here)**

4

7

Shechem

9

AMMON

8

Bethlehem

PHILISTIA

6

3

2

MOAB

1

5

LESSON 11

David Brings the Ark of the Covenant to Jerusalem (II Samuel 6)

In the days after David was anointed king over all Israel, from Dan to Beersheba, he gathered together all the chosen men of Israel, numbering thirty thousand. With these men, David arose to bring up the Ark of the Covenant from Baalejudah, where it had remained during the reign of Saul.

Along the way to Jerusalem, when they had carried the Ark of the Covenant six steps, David stopped and sacrificed an ox and a fatling to the Lord. And wearing only a linen ephod, David danced before the Lord with all his might. So David and all the house of Israel brought up the Ark of the Lord with shouting, and with the sound of the trumpet.

And as the Ark of the Lord came into the city of David, Michal, Saul's daughter and David's first wife, looked out her window and saw David leaping and dancing before the Lord; and she despised him in her heart.

And they brought in the Ark of the Lord, and set it in its place, in the midst of the tabernacle that David had set up for it, and David offered burnt offerings and peace offerings and blessed all the people of Israel in the name of the Lord of hosts. And all the people that had gathered in Jerusalem celebrated the return of the Ark of the Covenant, and David gave out cakes of bread and cakes of raisins before they returned to their homes.

Then David went to bless his household, and Michal, the daughter of Saul, came to meet him and said, "How glorious was the king of Israel today, who uncovered himself today before the eyes of the peoples' servants, as one of the vain young men shamelessly uncovers himself!"

To this insult, David responded and said to Michal, "It was before the Lord, who chose me above your father and his house to appoint me ruler over the people of the Lord and over all of Israel, therefore I will celebrate before the Lord. And I will become more undignified than this, and will be humble in my own eyes, and will be honored with the honor of the peoples' servants."

Thus, Michal, the daughter of Saul, had no child unto the day of her death.

God's Covenant with the House of David (II Samuel 7)

And it came to pass, when David the king sat on Israel's throne in his house, and the Lord gave him rest from all his enemies, that the king said to Nathan the prophet of God, "See now, I dwell in a house of cedar, but the Ark of the Covenant dwells in a tent."

And Nathan said to David, "Go and do what is in your heart, for the Lord is with you."

And the Word of the Lord came to Nathan that night, God said to Nathan, "Go and tell my servant David, thus says the Lord, will you build for me a house to dwell in?

I have not dwelled in a house since the time that I brought up the children of Israel from Egypt. When I went with the people, did I ever say to the tribes of Israel, 'Why have you not built me a house of cedar?'

Now tell my servant David, thus says the Lord of hosts, I took you from the pasture, from tending the sheep, to be ruler over my people Israel, and I was with you wherever you went and cut off all your enemies and made for you a great name, like the names of the greatest men on the earth. I will also give you rest from your enemies and make a house for you. And when your days are complete and you go to sleep with your fathers, I will establish your seed after you, which will come from you, and I will establish your kingdom. He shall build a house for my name, and I will establish the throne of his kingdom forever. I will be his father, and he shall be my son. If he commits iniquity, I will chasten him with the rod of men, and with the stripes of the children of men, but my mercy shall not depart from him, as I took it from Saul, and your house and your kingdom shall be established forever before you, your throne shall be established forever." According to all these words and to this vision, so did Nathan speak them to David.

Then King David went and sat before the Lord and said, "Who am I, O Lord God, that you have brought me this far? For the sake of your Word and according to your own heart, you have done great things to let your servant know. For this reason, you are great, O Lord God, for there is none like you, and there is no God besides you, and what nation on the earth is like your people Israel? For you have confirmed for yourself your people Israel to be a people for you forever, and you, Lord, have become their God.

And now, O Lord God, let the house of your servant David be established before you. Lord God, you are God, and your words are true, and you have promised this goodness to your servant, therefore let it please you to bless the house of your servant, that it may continue forever before you."

QUESTIONS

1. Who is the Lord making a promise to in these verses?
   God is making a promise to King David.

2. What is the "house" built for God's name? Who will build it?
   Solomon, David's son and heir to the throne, built the Temple for the Lord in Jerusalem.

3. How long will the descendants of David rule over God's people?
   Forever; God promised that David's house will always rule over the people.

4. Who is the last and greatest king of Israel sitting on an eternal throne?
   Though the throne of Israel was disgraced by wicked kings and ultimately lost its power, God sent His own son, Jesus, to be the King that would never lose his heavenly throne.

LESSON 11

BACKGROUND AND SUMMARY (Also read pp. 44-45.)

In this lesson, Saul completes his tragic descent and shows his severe disdain for the ways of God by seeking the insight of a witch, an act prohibited by the law of Moses. From the witch, he learns of the inevitable judgment God had planned for him. Second, Michal shows herself a spiritual child of Saul by disapproving of David's worship. For her unholy pride, the Lord refused to grant her children. Lastly, David's unhindered, unrestrained rejoicing at the return of the Ark of the Covenant further confirmed his sincere love for God. The Lord responded with a supreme gift that changed the remaining contour of the whole Bible.

David received the ultimate gift when the Lord made a special covenant with him and his line. God bestowed an eternal kingship. In other words, the kings from David's line would forever rule over and lead the people of God. This position is the most amazing responsibility ever given to men, and begs the question, who could ever fulfill such an important position?

Jesus Christ is the King of God's people that not only knew the law of Moses, but fulfilled it in his life and ministry on earth. When he had accomplished this ministry, he went to be with the Father and sat down at His right hand upon an eternal throne. From his throne, Christ will forever reign over all the Father has given him.

The story of this lesson is as follows:

- Saul inquires from a medium about how his battle with the Philistines will go.
- The Spirit of Samuel prophesies the death of Saul and his sons in the battle.
- Saul kills himself in the battle.
- David laments and writes a psalm for Saul and Jonathan.
- David is anointed and becomes king over Judah in Hebron. Abner makes Ishbosheth king over Israel.
- David becomes king over all Israel.

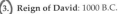

FACTS TO KNOW

1. **Witch of Endor**: summoned the spirit of Samuel
2. **Gilboa**: mountain where Saul and his sons died
3. **Reign of David**: 1000 B.C.
4. **City of David**: Jerusalem; where the Ark of the Covenant dwells
5. **Michal**: wife of David; despised him for dancing before the Ark of the Lord
6. **Nathan**: God's prophet to David
7. **Covenant with David**: God's promise to keep for the house of David an eternal throne

MEMORY VERSE

> **II SAMUEL 1:19-20**
>
> *The beauty of Israel is slain upon Thy high places: how are the mighty fallen!*
> *Tell it not in Gath, publish it not in the streets of Ashkelon; lest the daughters of the Philistines rejoice, lest the daughters of the uncircumcised triumph.*

1. What is "the beauty of Israel"?
   The royal family, Saul and his sons, especially Jonathan.

2. What does "slain upon the high places" mean?
   They were killed on Mt. Gilboa.

3. Who are the daughters of the Philistines? Who are the daughters of the uncircumcised?
   Both are the Philistine women, the enemies of Israel. The Philistine women sing songs about victory in battle, just as the Israelite women did about Saul and David.

4. Who are "the mighty fallen"?
   The same as the "beauty of Israel," Saul and Jonathan, who were once mighty but then fell to the Philistines in battle.

VOCABULARY AND EXPRESSIONS

1. **medium**: a person who communicates with the spirits of dead people through witchcraft. God forbids Israel to have anything to do with such practices (Leviticus 20:6, Deuteronomy 18:9-12).

2. **lament**: funeral song or dirge

3. **"he tore his clothes and fasted"**: physical expression of grief and mourning

COMPREHENSION QUESTIONS

1. What warning did Samuel give to Saul through the medium? _____ Samuel told Saul that in battle the following day, the Philistines would defeat the Israelites and Saul and his sons would be killed. (p. 248)

2. Why does the memory verse say, "Tell it not in Gath, publish it not in the streets of Ashkelon"? _____ Gath and Ashkelon are cities of the Philistines. The poet does not want the news to travel to these cities because they will rejoice that the king of Israel and his sons are dead.

3. How old was David when he was anointed king of Israel? How long did he reign? _____ David was 30 years old when he was anointed king. He reigned 40 years. (p. 252)

   Why was David so happy to bring the Ark up to Jerusalem? _____ Since the Philistines had captured and kept the Ark for many years, David was glad to have the symbol of God's presence back again with God's people. His joy and excitement caused him to worship God without caring what others thought. (pp. 44-45 of guide)

4. Why did Michal despise David's rejoicing and dancing? How did God punish her? _____ Michal worried too much about what people would say and she thought that David's rejoicing was not dignified enough for a king. For her pride, God did not permit her to conceive a child for David. (pp. 44-45 of guide)

5. What did David want to do for the Lord? What did the Lord promise to do for David instead? _____ David did not like the fact that he had a palace while the Ark stayed in a tent, and he wanted to build God a temple. Instead, God promised to make an everlasting house for David, a line of kings that would never pass away. (pp. 44-45 of guide)

GEOGRAPHY

1. Locate on your map and memorize:
   - ☐ Mt. Gilboa
   - ☐ Hebron
   - ☐ Jerusalem
2. Territories surrounding Israel conquered by David:
   - ☐ Philistia
   - ☐ Edom
   - ☐ Aram
   - ☐ Moab
   - ☐ Ammon
   - ☐ Phoenicia

BIG PICTURE OF THE BIBLE

- **Deuteronomy 17:14-20:** What kingly expectations did Moses put in the Law?
- **Psalm 2, 24, 45:1-7**, and **89:** How do these royal psalms praise the special place God gave to the house of David and also magnify Jesus' fulfillment of all kingly hopes?
- **Jeremiah 33:14-22; Ezekiel 37:24-28:** Who do the prophets say will return and accompany the spiritual restoration of Israel?
- **Luke 1:31-33:** What was Gabriel's message to Mary about her son's future reign?
- **Hebrews 1:** How are the royal psalms of David connected to the person of Jesus?
- **Revelation 20:11-21:7:** What is St. John's description of Jesus in this passage?

MEMORY WORK

Continue to review the Old Testament books (5-12-5-5-12).

GEOGRAPHY

Saul and the Spirit of Samuel:

- **Mt. Gilboa**, where Saul and Jonathan die, is south of **Jezreel**.

David the King:

- David first ruled in **Hebron**, north of **Beersheba**. He later moved to **Jerusalem** just north of **Bethlehem**.
- Six of the peoples David subdued lie around Israel; starting in the north and going clockwise: **Phoenicia, Aram, Ammon, Moab, Edom,** and **Philistia.**

ACTIVITIES

- pp. 248-249: Identify Saul and the medium. Why is Saul dressed like a commoner? What news is he learning from the medium?

  Saul has disguised himself like a common man so that he could visit the medium secretly. He is learning that God has given him, his sons, and his army over to defeat at the hands of the Philistines.

- pp. 250-251: What are the people doing in the picture? Who are they following? Where are they going?

  The people are following David to Jerusalem, because they want David to rule over Israel and be their king.

- p. 251: Reread David's poetic lament. Explain your selection(s) of your favorite line(s).
- Draw a picture from the lesson of:

  1. David's anointing as king by Israel's elders in Hebron
  2. David and the men of Israel carrying the Ark of the Covenant up to Jerusalem
  3. David praying to the Lord that He would bless the house of His servant

LESSON 12

BACKGROUND AND SUMMARY

Nearly ten years after taking control of Israel, David tarried at home when the fighting men left for a season of war. Interestingly, the biblical author supplies no rationale for David's staying behind in Jerusalem. Thus, we may conclude that David had no good reason for remaining and should have been with his men. Further, his choice to stay home from war became the opportunity for his great sin with Bathsheba. From this dark scene in David's life, we can glean two powerful lessons.

First, sin is not limited to just the wrong things we commit against God; but it is also the absence of doing right things for Him. In other words, we are more likely to fall into sin when we are not focused on doing the right things. In the case of David, he was probably not planning on staying home from war so that he could break the Sixth, Seventh, Ninth, and Tenth Commandments. But not being in the right place cost David dearly.

Second, temptation is no respecter of persons. In other words, the king of God's people can fall into sin just as easily as the next person. David probably was not expecting such temptation when he ventured on the roof that night, but he was guilty of not being prepared for dealing with it when it came. We must remember that from birth we have an inclination toward sin, not righteousness. It is our nature to be sinful, but we must remember that Christ has come to heal the sick, not the healthy. He will change our nature as we rely on Jesus' goodness and purity.

The story of the lesson is as follows:

- David captures Jerusalem, and he conquers the lands of the Philistines, Moab, and others.
- David finds Jonathan's son, Mephibosheth, and shows kindness.
- The Israelites go to fight Ammon, but David stays in Jerusalem.
- David falls in love with Bathsheba, and has her husband, Uriah, killed.
- Nathan accuses David with a parable, and David repents, but his infant son dies.
- Another son, Solomon, is born.

VOCABULARY AND EXPRESSIONS

1. **"lame on both his feet"**: unable to walk. In such archaic times, the care of a crippled person would be a very heavy burden upon his family.

2. **"such a dead dog as I am"**: statement of unworthiness and utter humility. Mephibosheth describes himself in the lowest terms possible.

3. **wayfarer**: traveler, stranger, sojourner. In ancient times, people relied desperately upon the hospitality of others when on a journey.

LESSON 12: David Finds Jonathan's Son | David and Bathsheba
Golden Children's Bible: pp. 252-255 (II Samuel 8, 9, 11-12)

FACTS TO KNOW

1. **Ziba**: servant of the house of Saul
2. **Mephibosheth**: Jonathan's lame son
3. **Joab**: general of David's army
4. **Bathsheba**: Uriah the Hittite's wife
5. **Uriah the Hittite**: faithful soldier in David's army; killed in battle
6. **Nathan**: delivered God's judgment over David
7. **fasting**: a period of prayer and self-denial

MEMORY VERSE

PSALM 19:1-3

The heavens declare the glory of God, the firmament showeth his handiwork. Day unto day uttereth speech, night unto night showeth knowledge. There is no speech or language where their voice is not heard.

1. How do the heavens "declare the glory of God"?
   The beauty and majesty of the heavens reflect the greatness of the Creator who made them.

2. What is "firmament"?
   Firmament is another word for the sky.

3. What does "day unto day" and "night unto night" mean?
   These expressions mean continually or all the time.

4. How do the heaven and sky speak every language?
   True beauty is a universal language and the beauty of God's creation is a language anyone and everyone can understand.

COMPREHENSION QUESTIONS

1. What areas surrounding Israel did the Lord give over into David's hand after David took over the throne in Israel? _David triumphed over and conquered the Philistines in the south, the Moabites in the east, and Hadadezer of the Arameans and the Syrians in the north._ (p. 252)

2. What request did David have for Ziba? _After his victories, David asked Ziba to locate anyone remaining from the house of Saul so that David could show him kindness as a measure of gratitude to his great friend, Jonathan._ (p. 253)

3. Who did Ziba find for David? What did David do for him? _Ziba found Jonathan's lame son, Mephibosheth. David restored his family lands and offered him a home in the royal palace._ (p. 253)

4. Why did David remain in Jerusalem when the men went off to war? _David did not have a good reason to stay in Jerusalem because the Bible records no reason._

5. What sin did David commit in order to have Bathsheba for himself? _David both deceived Uriah and gave the orders that brought about the murder of Uriah._ (p. 254)

6. Who confronted David about his sin? How did he bring David to see the wrong he had done? _Nathan exposed to David his great sin through telling a parable about an evil man that did something similar to the great evil David had done. When David wanted to know who the evil man was, Nathan explained boldly, "You are the man!"_ (p. 254)

7. What did David do when his son fell sick? _David prayed to God and fasted._ (p. 255)

BIG PICTURE OF THE BIBLE

- **Psalm 32:** Observe the way David describes his agony when he had not confessed his sin, and his joy that followed his repentance. David is assured that the Lord defends him.

- **Psalm 51:** Pay careful attention to the various spiritual lessons included in David's cries of remorse. In verse 4, David acknowledged that his sin was primarily an offense to his holy and just God. In verse 5, David admitted that his original nature was sinful. Rather than use this fact to excuse his sin, David recognized how great God's salvation was to restore and purify a person sinful from birth. Throughout the psalm (especially verses 2, 6, and 7), David envisioned God's forgiveness as much more than a surface restoration, but as thoroughly complete and penetrating into the depths of his soul. Lastly, David defined the true nature of repentance in verses 16-17 as not ritual observances and outward displays, but sincere, heartfelt remorse within one's soul. This psalm remains a great lesson for us on how to be restored to the Lord when we have failed him by sinning.

MEMORY WORK

Continue to review the Old Testament books (5-12-5-5-12).

ACTIVITIES

- pp. 252-253 Identify David. What is the city in the background?
  David is coming to his new home, Jerusalem, the city of Israelite kings.

- p. 254 Narrate the story Nathan told David.
  Nathan told David a parable about a rich man and a poor man. All the poor man had was a little lamb that was very precious to him. When the rich man had guests, he did not want to offer his livestock as a meal, so he took the poor man's lamb and served it instead. David was greatly offended by the rich man's crime.

- p. 255 Who are the man and woman in the picture? What is the woman doing?
  From his rooftop, David is watching Bathsheba as she bathes. He should never have looked there because his desire grew stronger as he lingered in watching her. David was able to get away with his sin because the incident happened at night. (II Samuel 11:2)

- What hope stopped David's mourning after the death of his child?
  David was confident that though his son could not come to him, he would someday go to his son. He meant that while father and son could not be reunited in this life, they would meet again in the next.

LESSON 13

BACKGROUND AND SUMMARY

In the story of David's sin with Bathsheba, we see an excellent example of a sinner's repentance and the Lord's restoration. The restoration of David after his sin, however, does not dismiss the consequences of that sin. In this next lesson, we can find another powerful truth embodied by the life of David: spiritual restoration does not guarantee physical deliverance. Consider the consequences of David's sin.

In II Samuel 12:10-12, Nathan pronounces to David that "the sword shall never depart from your house." In other words, David's house will be ruled by turmoil, strife, and unrest. Throughout the remainder of David's life, his family was torn apart by conspiracy, incest, murder, and deception. There remains no greater example of this than Absalom's revolt against his father. David's favorite son becomes his enemy in a vicious struggle for power over the kingdom. Absalom's life ends with tragedy upon tragedy.

In this horrible story, we can see how much one person's sin affects his family. David alone chose to sin in taking Uriah's wife, but David's whole family endured the consequences of those sins. Remember this: sin appears pleasing and insignificant at first, but it always proves more destructive than ever imagined. Having the foresight to envision the consequences will aid us greatly in resisting temptation.

The story of this lesson is as follows:

- Absalom steals the hearts of the people by judging for them.
- Absalom raises an army and plans to become king.
- David and his loyal subjects flee Jerusalem.
- The army of David defeats that of Absalom in the woods of Ephraim.
- Absalom is killed by Joab in the battle.
- David hears the news and weeps for Absalom.
- David instructs Solomon and then dies.

LESSON 13: David and Absalom | The Death of David
Golden Children's Bible: pp. 256-260 (II Samuel 14, 15, 18, 23; I Kings 2)

FACTS TO KNOW

1. **Absalom**: David's favorite son, most handsome in Israel
2. **Joab**: David's commander who killed Absalom
3. **Solomon**: David's son, the third king of Israel; wisest man of his time
4. **Bathsheba**: Solomon's mother

MEMORY VERSE

> **II SAMUEL 18:33**
>
> *O my son Absalom, my son, my son Absalom! would God I had died for thee, O Absalom, my son, my son!*

1. Who is speaking?
   David is crying out in grief for his son.

2. Why is the speaker in mourning for Absalom?
   For trying to take the throne from his father, Absalom has been killed by David's men.

3. What does "would God I had died for thee" mean?
   David wishes that God would have allowed him to be killed rather than his son.

VOCABULARY AND EXPRESSIONS

1. **"Absalom stole the hearts of the men of Israel."**: Absalom's winning ways and handsome good looks made him very popular with the people of the land.

2. **conspiracy**: a plot, scheme, or trick (from Latin *conspirare*, "to breathe together")

3. **"I go the way of all the earth"**: Like all living things in the world, he will soon die. David alludes to Genesis 3:19: "For you are dust, and to dust you shall return."

COMPREHENSION QUESTIONS

1. Why was war waged between Absalom and David? __Absalom made a conspiracy to seize__ control of Israel from Hebron and challenged the rule of his father. (p. 256)

2. How did David's people show their loyalty to David concerning the war? __The people would not__ let David lead his forces into battle. Rather, they allowed him to command from inside the city and vowed to obey his command. (p. 256)

3. How did Absalom die? __Joab stabbed him to death while he was caught in a tree. (p. 258)__

4. What instruction did David give to Solomon before he died? __David told his son that if God__ was going to fulfill His promises to the house of David, then Solomon must keep the commandments of God found in the Law of Moses. (p. 260)

5. What qualities did David tell the people a king should have? __The king must be just, ruling__ in the fear of God. He must be as the light on a clear morning, and he must be tender as the first grass coming up after a rain. (p. 260)

6. Who ruled after David? __Solomon ruled Israel after his father, David. (p. 260)__

GEOGRAPHY

1. Locate on your map and review:
   - ☐ Ephraim
   - ☐ Edom
   - ☐ Ammon
   - ☐ Aram
   - ☐ Phoenicia
   - ☐ Moab

BIG PICTURE OF THE BIBLE

- **Psalm 55:12-14:** See David's lament over the former companions that have betrayed him. Consider the detail of his indictment in verse 14.

MEMORY WORK

Continue to review the Old Testament books (5-12-5-5-12).

GEOGRAPHY

Identify the landscape of expanded Israelite lands under the united rule of the Davidic king. The borders of Israel grew to their greatest expanse during the reign of David. Review these six peoples conquered by David: **Phoenicia, Aram, Ammon, Moab, Edom,** and **Philistia.**

ACTIVITIES

- Who were the first three kings of Israel? Memorize them.
  Saul, David, Solomon

- p. 257: Identify Absalom. What is he doing in the picture?
  Absalom is hearing the people in the place of judgment, where he gained the favor of all Israel.

- pp. 258-259: Describe what has happened to Absalom in the picture.
  Absalom was caught in a tree, lost his horse, and found himself in a very compromising position.

- p. 260: Who is on the deathbed? Who is the boy next to him?
  Solomon attends to his dying father and waits to hear David's final instructions.

LESSON 14

BACKGROUND AND SUMMARY

In the figure of Solomon, we see both the greatest fulfillment of God's blessings for national Israel and the firstfruits of her demise. From Solomon, we may glean two valuable lessons.

First, blessing always extends beyond the original recipient. In this way, God's material blessings for Israel were given for the greater purpose of drawing the nations to Israel's God. As Moses had foretold, Israel achieved a reputation in the Ancient Near East for her material and spiritual greatness. Solomon embodied this greatness with his unmatched wisdom and extravagant beautification of Jerusalem. By the example of the Queen of Sheba, we see that the nations connected Solomon's fame with the renown of the Lord's name. In other words, Israel's preeminence was the direct result of her relationship with the Lord of hosts, Yahweh, the greatest of all gods. Unfortunately, Solomon is both the apex of Israel's excellence and her initial point of descent.

Secondly, in the words of Jesus, to whom much is given, much is required. In other words, the increase of blessing always means an increase in responsibility. Tragically, Solomon did not understand fully the weight of this truth. As Solomon grew in fame and prestige throughout the known world, he began to flirt with the pagan religions of his numerous concubines. His flirtations soon led to tolerance and eventually full acceptance, which meant covenant infidelity. Interestingly, the consistent metaphor of marital unfaithfulness, used over and over in the Old Testament to describe the disrupted relationship between God and his people, was acted out by Solomon with his 700 wives and 300 concubines! Thus, Solomon traded the responsibilities of God's king for the pleasures of a worldly despot.

The story of this lesson is as follows:

- Solomon asks God for an understanding heart to judge His people.
- God gave him wisdom as well as riches and honor over all other kings of his day.
- Solomon shows his wisdom by judging between two women. His fame spreads.
- Solomon builds the Temple.
- The Queen of Sheba visits and tests Solomon.
- Because Solomon turns to other gods, God divides the kingdom between Jeroboam and Rehoboam.

FACTS TO KNOW

1. **the Temple**: center of Israel's worship; permanent house for the Ark of God
2. **Queen of Sheba**: tested Solomon with hard questions
3. **Sheba**: ancient Arabian kingdom; present-day Yemen; colonized Ethiopia
4. **Division of Israel**: 931 B.C.; when Israel split into the Northern and Southern kingdoms
5. **Jeroboam**: son of Solomon's servant; ruled Israel
6. **Rehoboam**: Solomon's son; reigned over Judah
7. **Ahijah**: prophet of God to Jeroboam

MEMORY VERSE

> **I KINGS 10:1**
>
> *And when the queen of Sheba heard of the fame of Solomon concerning the name of the Lord, she came to prove him with hard questions.*

1. What is the fame of Solomon?
   Israel was known throughout the world for the wealth and insight of Solomon.

2. What does "prove him" mean?
   "Prove him" means to test him. She wanted to see if Solomon was as wise as she had heard.

3. What is it about the fame of Solomon that so interests the queen?
   More than just the insights of Solomon, the queen wanted to learn more about the God that granted Solomon his wisdom.

VOCABULARY AND EXPRESSIONS

1. **"holy of holies"**: the innermost part of the Tabernacle or Temple that contained only the Ark of the Covenant, the place where God's presence dwelled. The high priest of Israel would only enter this most sacred place once a year on the Day of Atonement.

2. **cherubim**: the winged angelic creatures that adorn the Ark of the Covenant and attend the Lord in heavenly worship.

COMPREHENSION QUESTIONS

1. What did Solomon ask God to grant him? What did he receive? __Solomon requested an__ understanding heart that he might be a fair judge of his people. God granted him riches and honor along with wisdom. (p. 262)

2. Describe the argument between the women who presented their case to Solomon. __One woman__ whose baby had died was accused by the other of switching the dead baby for her live baby. (pp. 263-264)

3. How did Solomon resolve the dispute? __He threatened to kill the child, causing the real__ mother to reveal herself by agreeing to give up the baby rather than killing it. (p. 264)

4. Describe the temple Solomon built to the Lord. How long did it take to build? __It was 90 feet__ long, 30 feet wide, 45 feet high, with a broad portico in front, narrow windows, many chambers, walls of stone, floor and ceiling of cedar, floor covered in fir, covered in gold and decorated with gold-covered figures. It took seven years to build. (pp. 265-267)

5. What was placed in the Temple? __Ritual objects were placed in the temple, including the__ Ark of the Covenant. (pp. 266-267)

6. Why did the Lord become displeased with Solomon? What became of Solomon's kingdom? __Solomon became too devoted to riches; he performed sacrifices and rituals to other gods, so the Lord divided his kingdom in half, giving Jeroboam control of the northern half. (pp. 268-269)

GEOGRAPHY

1. Locate on your map and memorize:
   - ☐ The Northern Kingdom   ☐ The Southern Kingdom   ☐ Sheba

   Judah:
   - ☐ Jerusalem

   Israel:
   - ☐ Shechem   ☐ Dan   ☐ Bethel

BIG PICTURE OF THE BIBLE

- **John 8:2-11:** Like Solomon did in I Kings 3:16-18, where does Jesus say his wisdom originates?
- **Matthew 12:6, John 2:19:** What does Jesus say about the Temple? Why?
- **I Corinthians 3:16, 6:19:** What does Paul teach about God, by His Spirit, dwelling in the temple of His people?
- **Revelation 21:22:** What does John say will not be in heaven?
- **Luke 11:31:** With whom does Jesus contrast the Queen of Sheba?

MEMORY WORK

Continue to review the Old Testament books (5-12-5-5-12).

GEOGRAPHY

In 931 B.C., Israel divided into a Northern and Southern kingdom. This division affected the significance of several locations within Israel's territory. Identify the new borders of each kingdom and the important cities and religious centers:

- **The Northern Kingdom (Israel)** is the shaded area with **Bethel** at its southernmost end and **Dan** at its northernmost. **Shechem** was its first capital.
- **Jerusalem** was the capital city of the **Southern Kingdom (Judah)**.
- **Sheba** was a country located far to the SE of Israel.

ACTIVITIES

- Read Solomon's prayer of dedication for the Temple in I Kings 8.
- pp. 262-263: Identify Solomon. Which woman is the baby's real mother? What is happening to the baby? Solomon judges the people from his throne. The true mother desperately pleads to Solomon for the child to live.
- pp. 266-267: Describe the Temple, including the structure, the walls, and the courtyards. The Temple contains walls that enclose courtyards that surround the Holy Place.
- p. 269: Identify the Queen of Sheba and Solomon. What is she doing? Identify the gifts that the queen brought Solomon, and the people and animals of her company that she brought with her. The Queen of Sheba has brought gifts of spices, gold, and precious stones to reward Solomon for his unmatched wisdom. Her servants come from Africa, bringing with them camels and elephants.
- **Copybook Verse Review:** #32-34 in Appendix.

LESSON 15

BACKGROUND AND SUMMARY

When the idolatry of Solomon grew too destructive, the Lord began a new project with Jeroboam. To him, God gave ten tribes and held out a promise of blessing and support if Jeroboam would restore covenant loyalty in the land. The record of Jeroboam's rule, and nearly all of the subsequent kings, including those in Judah, testifies to the utter failure of those projects. What had become of God's plan of redemption? How could He make a people for Himself out of such failures?

God reminded His true people that hope still remained. Hope is the central theme of Elijah's life—a hope against great odds. In the life of this prophet, we see some astounding contrasts that attest to God's amazing faithfulness. Let us consider two instances.

First, God will sustain His people. Both times Elijah fled for his life, God sent miraculous forms of physical and spiritual sustenance to preserve him. Even when Elijah despaired to the point of considering suicide, God encouraged His prophet through remarkable manifestations of His Spirit. Thus, Elijah knew that though no one in Israel seemed to care for him, the Lord would care for him faithfully. We can trust that when we feel alone in serving the Lord, He will sustain and comfort us by His Spirit.

Second, God will not leave His people without a testimony. In Elijah's life, God supplied a powerful testimony of His greatness to show up the prophets of Baal. Presently, we have an even greater demonstration of the Lord's might in the humble sacrifice of Christ that completely defeated the powers of sin, death, and the Devil. All other hopes are as foolish as calling on Baal, because Jesus is the true and living God.

The story of this lesson is as follows:

- God sends a drought. He provides for Elijah by ravens and a widow.
- Elijah heals the widow's son. He defeats and kills the prophets of Baal.
- Jezebel vows to kill Elijah, so he flees to Mt. Horeb. God speaks to him with reassurance and tells him to anoint Hazael, Jehu, and Elisha.

FACTS TO KNOW

1. **Israel**: Northern Kingdom after division
2. **Judah**: Southern Kingdom after division
3. **Ahab**: wicked and idolatrous king of Israel
4. **Jezebel**: Ahab's wife; daughter of a pagan king
5. **Baal**: pagan god worshiped by Ahab and Jezebel
6. **Elijah**: prophet of the Lord
7. **Gilead**: mountainous region east of the Jordan River
8. **Mt. Carmel**: where Elijah defeated the prophets of Baal
9. **widow**: a woman whose husband has died

MEMORY VERSE

> **I KINGS 19:11-12**
>
> *But the Lord was not in the wind: and after the wind an earthquake; but the Lord was not in the earthquake. And after the earthquake a fire; but the Lord was not in the fire: and after the fire a still, small voice.*

1. What is a "still small voice"?
   It is the sound of a slight breeze or breath.

2. What does Elijah experience that the Lord did not choose as a means of revealing himself?
   In this story, the Lord did not use worldly phenomena to speak to his prophet.

3. Where can the "still small voice" be heard?
   The still, small voice can be heard in the heart.

VOCABULARY AND EXPRESSIONS

- **Baalim** (ba a **leem**): plural form of Baal, Hebrew. Not another god, the Baalim are a host of separate Baals.
- **"Take away my life, for I am no better than my fathers."**: The persistent idolatry of Israel caused Elijah to despair to the point of death. He began to doubt whether or not his ministry as a prophet was accomplishing anything in turning back to God the unfaithful generations of Israel.
- **"still small voice"**: In great contrast to the powerful physical demonstrations of wind, earthquakes, and fire on the mountain, God directed Elijah by speaking in a soft, gentle way. Though Elijah may have wanted God to assert Himself in bold forms of judgment like an earthquake, God was instead showing mercy to Israel. In the same way, today Jesus calls us to his gospel with the Holy Spirit's gentle voice of mercy.
- **mantle**: cloak, outer garment

1. When did the division of the united kingdom of Israel occur? __931 B.C. (p. 270; the GCB gives__ a date of 922 B.C., but 931 B.C.—or a date range—is more widely accepted)

2. How did the Lord provide for the prophet Elijah during the famine? __God sent ravens to feed__ Elijah at Cherith, and sent him to the widow's house in Zarephath. (pp. 270-271)

3. What miracle did Elijah perform for the widow? __After the widow's son perished from a__ sickness, Elijah prayed to God, and the Lord revived the widow's son. (p. 271)

4. How did Elijah challenge the prophets of Baal at Mt. Carmel? Why? __Elijah said both he__ and the priests of Baal should prepare a sacrifice but start no fire. Then they should each ask their god to produce fire. This was a test to show who was the true and living God. (p. 272)

5. How was the three-year famine ended? __That evening after Elijah wiped out the__ prophets of Baal, the Lord sent the rains and ended the famine. (p. 275)

6. How did God present himself to Elijah at Mt. Horeb? What instructions did God give him? ____ The Lord revealed himself to Elijah in a still, small voice and instructed him to anoint a new king in Syria and Israel, and find Elisha, the prophet, to continue in his place. Thus, God was not ready to send catastrophic judgment on the land. (p. 276)

GEOGRAPHY

1. Identify on your map these important locations in the life of Elijah, and tell what took place at each:

☐ Samaria __capital of Ahab and Jezebel's Israel__

☐ Gilead __Elijah's home__

☐ Zarephath __where the widow received__ her son back

☐ Mt. Carmel __where Elijah defeated the__ prophets of Baal

☐ Beersheba __where Elijah fled from Ahab__ and Jezebel

☐ Mt. Horab __where Elijah heard the still,__ small voice

Lesson 15: Elijah and the Priests of Baal | The Still Small Voice   55

BIG PICTURE OF THE BIBLE

- **I Kings 18:27:** See the insults that Elijah gave to Baal when he would not answer the prophets. Other translations render his jabs more comically.
- **Matthew 17:1-13:** See Elijah's appearance during the Transfiguration of Jesus. Israel believed that Elijah would appear before the Messiah comes, and Jesus explains that a prophet like Elijah, John the Baptist, had already announced his coming (see Malachi 4:5 and Matthew 11:7-19).

MEMORY WORK

Continue to review the Old Testament books (5-12-5-5-12).

GEOGRAPHY

Pay special attention to the places Elijah traveled in the stories from this lesson. Review all the locations on the map to prepare for the upcoming Review Lesson and Test.

- By the time of Ahab's reign, Israel's capital had been moved to **Samaria,** just NW of **Shechem.**
- **Gilead,** Elijah's home, was east of the Jordan above **Ammon.**
- Elijah was recieved by the widow in **Zarephath,** a city of **Phoenicia.**
- At **Mt. Carmel,** south of **Zarephath** along the shore, Elijah opposed Baal's prophets.
- Fleeing Jezebel, Elijah went to **Beersheba,** and then to **Mt. Horeb** in the far southwest.

ACTIVITIES

- pp. 272-275: The prophets of Baal look very foolish praying so intently to a god that does not exist. Describe the disturbing practices they use to worship Baal. How did Elijah taunt and tease them when their god did not show up?

The prophets of Baal were so serious about their false religion that they would even cut themselves to prove their loyalty to Baal. This story is a good example of how strange false worship can become. Elijah comically pointed out the obvious: Baal is no god at all!

REVIEW LESSON: Unit 3

INSTRUCTIONS

Use the Review Lesson to support mastery of the material presented in the previous five lessons. Drill the Facts to Know orally or have a Facts to Know Bee. Students may also write a description next to each fact on a separate piece of paper. Places to Know should be identified on the map at the end of this lesson. Students may work independently or with the teacher to complete the exercises. A test for this unit is included in the back of this book.

REVIEW LESSON: Unit 3 (Lessons 11-15)

SALVATION HISTORY

United Kingdom of David
Death of the King
The Ark Returns to Jerusalem
God's Covenant with David
David Takes Another Man's Wife
A Son's Revolt
Israel Builds the Temple

Divided Kingdom of David
Formation of Israel
Formation of Judah
Most Wicked King and
Queen Come to Power
God's Showdown with Baal

Dates to Know
1000 B.C.
931 B.C.

Words to Know/Vocabulary
firmament: sky
parable: a story or fable that contains an important truth
fasting: period of prayer and self-denial
widow: a woman who has lost her husband
Baal: any pagan god of the Canaanites
Baalim: many pagan gods of the Canaanites
altar: stone and wood structure built for making burnt offerings and sacrifices
still small voice: a breeze or breath of air; soft word

People to Know
Witch of Endor
Nathan
Ziba
Mephibosheth
Joab
Bathsheba
Uriah
Absalom
Solomon
Queen of Sheba
Jeroboam
Rehoboam
Ahijah
Ahab
Jezebel
Elijah
David
Michal
Samuel
Saul

Places to Know
Aram
Beersheba
Bethel
Dan
Edom
Ephraim
Gilead
Hebron
Jerusalem
Mount Carmel
Mount Gilboa
Mount Horeb
Phoenicia
Samaria
Sheba
The Northern Kingdom (Israel)
The Southern Kingdom (Judah)
Zarephath

Books of the O.T.
5-12-5-5-12
Genesis
Exodus
Leviticus
Numbers
Deuteronomy

Joshua
Judges
Ruth
I, II Samuel
I, II Kings
I, II Chronicles
Ezra
Nehemiah
Esther

Job
Psalms
Proverbs
Ecclesiastes
Song of Solomon

Isaiah
Jeremiah
Lamentations
Ezekiel
Daniel

Hosea
Joel
Amos
Obadiah
Jonah
Micah
Nahum
Habakkuk
Zephaniah
Haggai
Zechariah
Malachi

Give the corresponding word or phrase:

1. He told Saul that he and his sons would die in battle. ___the spirit of Samuel___

2. the year David's reign as king of Israel began ___1000 B.C.___

3. David brought this to Jerusalem. ___Ark of the Covenant___

4. She despised David's celebrations and dancing. ___Michal___

5. God promised this to David with a covenant. ___an eternal throne___

6. God's prophet to David ___Nathan___

7. the descendants of David ___the house of David___

8. David conquered these nations. ___Philistia, Moab, Edom, Ammon, Aram, Syria, Phoenicia___

9. Jonathan's lame son ___Mephibosheth___

10. When the men went out to battle, David still tarried in ___Jerusalem___

11. She was the wife that David took from Uriah. ___Bathsheba___

12. the general of David's army ___Joab___

13. He told David a parable about a rich man and a poor man. ___Nathan___

14. David's son that led a revolt against his father ___Absalom___

15. This enemy of David's was caught in a tree and stabbed to death. ___Absalom___

16. David's son that inherited the throne ___Solomon___

17. This made Solomon world-famous. ___his great wisdom___

18. She brought Solomon questions and gifts from a distant land. ___Queen of Sheba___

19. This was the center of Israel's worship. ___the Temple___

20. three kings of Israel's united kingdom ___Saul, David, Solomon___

21. the date Israel was divided between North and South ___931 B.C.___

22. He was given control of the Northern kingdom. ___Jeroboam___

23. He ruled Judah—the Southern kingdom. ___Rehoboam___

24. God's prophet to Jeroboam ___Ahijah___

25. God's prophet that called for famine on Israel because of Ahab's sin ___Elijah___

OLD TESTAMENT DRILL QUESTIONS

The drill questions from Christian Studies I have been compiled in the Appendix. These questions will be used in each of the subsequent study guides for Christian Studies. Continue reviewing these as the year progresses.

REVIEW LESSON: Unit 3

TIMELINE REVIEW

Review the Big Picture of the Bible, so students understand the major periods (i.e., Creation, Patriarchs, Exodus, etc.). When they understand the periods, continue filling in the Full Timeline in the Appendix and populate each period with the important people. In this way, they will associate each person with the right events. (Example: Moses = Exodus)

Match up the Words to Know:

_D_ 1. parable
_G_ 2. fasting
_B_ 3. widow
_A_ 4. firmament
_F_ 5. Baalim
_C_ 6. altar
_E_ 7. still, small voice

A. sky
B. wife who lost her husband
C. structure for sacrifices
D. story with a truth
E. soft word
F. many pagan gods
G. period of prayer and self-denial

SALVATION HISTORY TIMELINE

Put these events in the correct order.

United Kingdom of David

_2_ The Ark Returns to Jerusalem
_6_ Israel Builds the Temple
_1_ Death of King Saul
_4_ David Takes Another Man's Wife
_3_ God's Covenant with David
_5_ A Son's Revolt

Divided Kingdom

_10_ God's Showdown with Baal
_8_ Formation of Judah
_7_ Formation of Israel
_9_ Most Wicked King and Queen Come to Power

Answer these comprehension questions from the lessons.

1. What did the Lord promise to do for David? ___God promised to make an everlasting house___ for David, a line of kings that would never pass away.

2. What sin did David commit in order to have Bathsheba for himself? ___David both deceived Uriah___ and gave the orders that brought about the murder of Uriah. (p. 254)

3. What instruction did David give to Solomon before he died? ___David told his son that if God___ was going to fulfill His promises to the house of David, then Solomon must keep the commandments of God found in the Law of Moses. (p. 260)

4. What did Solomon ask of God, and what was he given? ___Solomon requested an___ understanding heart that he might be a fair judge of his people. God granted him riches and honor along with wisdom. (p. 262)

5. What challenge did Elijah give to the prophets of Baal at Mt. Carmel? ___Elijah said both he and___ the priests of Baal should prepare a sacrifice but start no fire. Then they should each ask their god to produce fire. This was a test to show who was the true and living God. (p. 272)

SCRIPTURE MEMORIZATION

Check each box if you can recite the Scripture verse from memory. Write each from memory or teacher dictation. Be accurate.

☐ II Samuel 1:19-20 _____ The beauty of Israel is slain upon Thy high places: how are the mighty fallen! Tell it not in Gath, publish it not in the streets of Ashkelon; lest the daughters of the Philistines rejoice, lest the daughters of the uncircumcised triumph.

_____

☐ Psalm 19:1-3 _____ The heavens declare the glory of God, the firmament showeth his handiwork. Day unto day uttereth speech, night unto night showeth knowledge. There is no speech or language where their voice is not heard.

_____

☐ II Samuel 18:33 _____ O my son Absalom, my son, my son Absalom! would God I had died for thee, O Absalom, my son, my son!

_____

☐ I Kings 10:1 _____ And when the queen of Sheba heard of the fame of Solomon concerning the name of the Lord, she came to prove him with hard questions.

_____

☐ I Kings 19:11-12 _____ But the Lord was not in the wind: and after the wind an earthquake; but the Lord was not in the earthquake. And after the earthquake a fire; but the Lord was not in the fire: and after the fire a still, small voice.

_____

MEMORY VERSES

To recite memory verses, give the first few words and let students complete the verse orally. Students should write the verse from memory or copy it from the lesson.

BOOKS OF THE OLD TESTAMENT

The Books of the Law

1. Genesis
2. Exodus
3. Leviticus
4. Numbers
5. Deuteronomy

The Books of History

1. Joshua
2. Judges
3. Ruth
4. I Samuel
5. II Samuel
6. I Kings
7. II Kings
8. I Chronicles
9. II Chronicles
10. Ezra
11. Nehemiah
12. Esther

The Books of Wisdom

1. Job
2. Psalms
3. Proverbs
4. Ecclesiastes
5. Song of Solomon

The Books of the Major Prophets

1. Isaiah
2. Jeremiah
3. Lamentations
4. Ezekiel
5. Daniel

The Books of the Minor Prophets

1. Hosea
2. Joel
3. Amos
4. Obadiah
5. Jonah
6. Micah
7. Nahum
8. Habakkuk
9. Zephaniah
10. Haggai
11. Zechariah
12. Malachi

MORE REVIEW EXERCISES

The following exercises will test your knowledge of important facts and history so far.

Put the following periods in Salvation History in the correct order:

4	Conquest of Canaan	8	Divided Kingdom
3	Exodus	2	Patriarchs
1	Prehistory	7	United Kingdom of David
5	Period of the Judges	6	Reign of Saul

Match the acts of Creation with each day:

D	Day One	**A.**	air and sea animals
E	Day Two	**B.**	dry land, seas, plants
B	Day Three	**C.**	day of rest
G	Day Four	**D.**	night and day
A	Day Five	**E.**	sky (Heaven)
F	Day Six	**F.**	land animals, humans
C	Day Seven	**G.**	sun and moon

Match each character name with its meaning:

D	Eve	**A.**	I will praise
F	Abraham	**B.**	mother of nations and kings
B	Sarah	**C.**	drawn out
E	Isaac	**D.**	mother of all living
A	Judah	**E.**	he who laughs
C	Moses	**F.**	father of nations

REVIEW LESSON: Unit 3

List the ten plagues in order.

1. Plague of water and blood
2. Plague of frogs
3. Plague of lice
4. Plague of flies
5. Plague of cattle
6. Plague of sores
7. Plagues of hail and fire
8. Plague of locusts
9. Plague of darkness
10. Death of the firstborn

List the twelve tribes of Israel.

1. Reuben
2. Simeon
3. Levi
4. Judah
5. Issachar
6. Zebulun
7. Gad
8. Asher
9. Dan
10. Naphthali
11. Joseph
12. Benjamin

MAP WORK

Places to Know

- ☐ Aram
- ☐ Beersheba
- ☐ Bethel
- ☐ Dan
- ☐ Edom
- ☐ Ephraim
- ☐ Gilead
- ☐ Hebron
- ☐ Jerusalem
- ☐ Mount Carmel
- ☐ Mount Gilboa
- ☐ Mount Horeb
- ☐ Phoenicia
- ☐ Samaria
- ☐ Sheba
- ☐ The Northern Kingdom (Israel)
- ☐ The Southern Kingdom (Judah)
- ☐ Zarephath

We recommend that the student first locate and highlight the place to know on the labeled map, then find it and add place names to the blank map during a geography test or drill.

UNIT 3 MAP A

Zarephath

ARAM

PHOENICIA

Dan

Mt. Carmel

Jezreel

Mt. Gilboa

Jordan River

Gilead

Samaria

Shechem

AMMON

EPHRAIM

Bethel

Jerusalem

Bethlehem

PHILISTIA

Hebron

Beersheba

The Northern Kingdom
The Southern Kingdom

MOAB

EDOM

SHEBA

Mt. Horeb

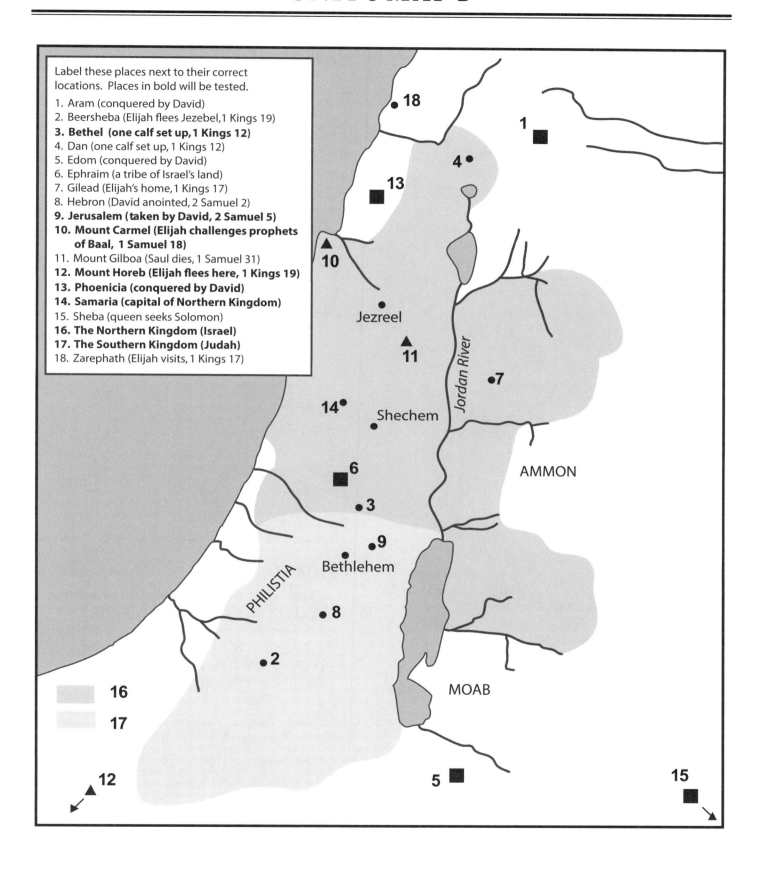

Label these places next to their correct locations. Places in bold will be tested.

1. Aram (conquered by David)
2. Beersheba (Elijah flees Jezebel, 1 Kings 19)
3. **Bethel (one calf set up, 1 Kings 12)**
4. Dan (one calf set up, 1 Kings 12)
5. Edom (conquered by David)
6. Ephraim (a tribe of Israel's land)
7. Gilead (Elijah's home, 1 Kings 17)
8. Hebron (David anointed, 2 Samuel 2)
9. **Jerusalem (taken by David, 2 Samuel 5)**
10. **Mount Carmel (Elijah challenges prophets of Baal, 1 Samuel 18)**
11. Mount Gilboa (Saul dies, 1 Samuel 31)
12. **Mount Horeb (Elijah flees here, 1 Kings 19)**
13. **Phoenicia (conquered by David)**
14. **Samaria (capital of Northern Kingdom)**
15. Sheba (queen seeks Solomon)
16. **The Northern Kingdom (Israel)**
17. **The Southern Kingdom (Judah)**
18. Zarephath (Elijah visits, 1 Kings 17)

Jezreel

Jordan River

Shechem

AMMON

Bethlehem

PHILISTIA

MOAB

LESSON 16

BACKGROUND AND SUMMARY

God's message to Elijah on Mt. Horeb was not the word of judgment that the prophet had expected. Rather, the Lord instructed him to anoint a new king over Israel and another prophet to carry on his own ministry. In other words, God was not ready to judge Israel for her wickedness.

The tragic account of Naboth's murder revealed the true extent of Ahab and Jezebel's perversion of the kingly ministry. When the king should have been leading the people in their observance of God's law, he was instead seizing the family lands of a humble vinedresser through gross treachery. Ahab was the anti-king, because he was a king worse than all the nations had.

Also, the unfortunate episode of Gehazi's deception and selfishness displayed how weakened the office of prophet had become. When the king failed in leading the people, the faithful remnant looked to the prophets to hear from God. But if the people cannot rely on the prophets, is there any hope left for Israel?

Though the scene appears quite bleak, there is a flickering flame of hope left in Israel. Elijah had fed that flame for many years, and at the time of his departure, the torch was passed to Elisha. Equipped with and empowered by the Spirit of God, Elisha at least would shoulder the ministry of the prophets in uncertain times. This dismal period of the kings may not offer us much encouragement when we suffer some of the same failures under our leaders. We must remember, however, not to place our hope in mere men, but rather trust that God is still at work through his faithful servants all around us. Men will fail us, but God cannot.

The story of this lesson is as follows:

- Ahab offers to buy Naboth's vineyard, but Naboth refuses.
- Jezebel orders Naboth's murder.
- Elijah prophesies Ahab's ruin and Jezebel's death.
- Elijah parts on a chariot of fire.
- Elisha heals the water, a leper, and Naaman. Gehazi deceives Naaman, and he is cursed by Elisha.

LESSON 16: Naboth's Vineyard | The Parting of Elijah and Elisha
Golden Children's Bible: pp. 278-283 (I Kings 21, II Kings 2, 5)

FACTS TO KNOW

1. **Samaria**: capital of Israel
2. **Naboth**: innocent vinedresser
3. **sackcloth and ashes**: worn during times of mourning
4. **Jordan River**: where Elijah was taken up to heaven
5. **Elisha**: prophet that took the place of Elijah
6. **Naaman**: captain of Syrian army; a leper, cured by Elisha
7. **leper**: someone who suffers from leprosy, a contagious disease; usually quarantined
8. **Gehazi**: selfish servant of Elisha

MEMORY VERSE

> **II KINGS 2:11**
> *There appeared a chariot of fire and horses of fire, and Elijah went up by a whirlwind into heaven.*

1. Describe Elijah's ascent in heaven.
   Elijah rode a heavenly, flaming chariot up in a rush of tornadic wind into the sky.

2. Who assumes Elijah's responsibilities on earth?
   Elisha took up the mantle of Elijah, in more than one way.

3. What is the significance of the Elijah's glorious whirlwind into heaven?
   Elijah had faithfully served the Lord as a prophet through very difficult times. Never experiencing death was his reward for such faithful service. Also, in this way, Elisha's wish to have a double portion of Elijah's spirit would be granted.

VOCABULARY AND EXPRESSIONS

1. **"The Lord forbid that I should give you the land which I have inherited from my forefathers."**: In Israel, land was the single most precious possession a person had, because God had given each family their portion of the Promised Land when Joshua divided the land among the Twelve Tribes.

2. **"sons of Belial"**: sons of the Devil; worthless men with no conscience for injustice or wrong

3. **vinedresser**: a person who tends and prunes grapevines

MEMORY VERSE

Because the memory verse for this lesson is brief, encourage the students to look ahead and begin work on next week's verse as it comprises a whole psalm.

COMPREHENSION QUESTIONS

1. What injustice did Jezebel commit regarding Naboth? Why? __In order to gain Naboth's__ vineyard for Ahab, Jezebel falsely accused him of blasphemy and had him stoned to death. (p. 278)

2. What punishment did God foretell for Jezebel and Ahab through Elijah? __Because Ahab mourned__ his sin, God waited to bring evil on their posterity. (p. 279)

3. What did Elisha ask of Elijah before he departed? __Elisha requested a double portion of__ Elijah's spirit. (p. 280)

4. How would Elisha know if his request was granted? __If Elisha could see Elijah as he__ departed the earth, his wish would be granted. (p. 280)

5. What miracle did Elisha first perform as a prophet? __He purified Jericho's water. (p. 280)__

6. What instructions did Elisha give Naaman to cure himself? __Elisha instructed the leper to bathe__ himself seven times in the Jordan River. (p. 282)

7. Why did Gehazi contract Naaman's leprosy? __Gehazi deceived Naaman into giving him__ the gifts that Naaman had brought for Elisha. (p. 283)

GEOGRAPHY

1. Locate the important places for the lesson on your map, and tell the significance:

☐ Samaria __capital of Ahab's Northern Kingdom__

☐ Syria __Naaman's country, north of Israel__

Lesson 16: Naboth's Vineyard I The Parting of Elijah and Elisha   **67**

BIG PICTURE OF THE BIBLE

- **I Kings 13:** See the account of another unfaithful prophet of God. Compare verses 6 and 33 and discuss how the failure of the prophet may be related to the continued failures of the king.
- **II Kings 2:23-24:** See another example of how God had anointed and empowered Elisha to prophesy to Israel. Notice how God was already foreshadowing the judgment that would come if the people continued to forsake His prophet(s).

MORE ACTIVITIES

Challenge the students to identify the two other men of God in the Old Testament that avoided a normal death like Elijah.

- **Enoch:** After walking with God all his life, Enoch was taken to heaven without having to see death (Genesis 5:24, Hebrews 11:5).
- **Moses:** After viewing the Promised Land, Moses passed away alone on Mt. Nebo, and God Himself buried him (Deut. 34:4-6).

GEOGRAPHY

- **Samaria** was the capital of Israel, where Ahab and Jezebel reigned.
- **Syria** was the home country of Naaman.

ACTIVITIES

- pp. 278-279: Identify Naboth and Ahab. Why would a king desire a humble vinedresser's only land? What does this tell you about the kind of person King Ahab was?

  Ahab had grown inordinately greedy. This story shows us how wicked Ahab had become by coveting the farmer's land and letting him be murdered for it.

- p. 281: Describe what is going on in the picture. Where are these men? What has Elijah left behind that Elisha will keep as his own?

  Elijah and Elisha have gathered at the Jordan River, where Elijah is taken up in a chariot of fire. Elisha will take up Elijah's mantle and wear it now that he will serve as a prophet for the Lord.

- p. 282: What is happening in this picture? Where is he?

  Naaman is bathing in the Jordan River.

- p. 283: Identify Elisha and Naaman. What does Naaman have for Elisha? What does Elisha say to the captain?

  Naaman has brought gifts for Elisha, but he refuses them.

LESSON 17

BACKGROUND AND SUMMARY

Amid the political struggles and upheaval that characterizes the period of the Kings, we see brief instances of God's judgment that serve as powerful warnings to the people. During the long stages of national apostasy (the Wilderness Wanderings, the period of the Judges, and the demise of Israel's kings), God extends to His people small intimations of the future major judgment to come, the Exile. Unfortunately, many of those warnings did not produce any lasting response.

One such warning comes in the form of Jehu's swift strict justice on the house of Ahab. Foreseen by the prophets, God exacted His judgment on Ahab's line through Jehu's purge of the royal house and Baal worship in Israel (II Kings 9-10). Why did Israel not see the warnings in these things?

Though the executions of Ahab's family and the worshipers of Baal may seem harsh to us now, we should remember that God takes very seriously the covenant He made with Israel. While Jehu's purges were a drastic measure of judgment, they cannot compare with the horrors visited upon the whole nation during the events surrounding the Exile.

The story of this lesson is as follows:

FACTS TO KNOW

1. **Jehu**: anointed king of Israel by Elisha's prophet; set to punishing Ahab's line
2. **Joram**: king of Israel; Ahab's son
3. **Ahaziah**: king of Judah; Ahab's grandson
4. **Athaliah**: Joram's widow and Ahaziah's mother; ruled as queen of Judah for seven years
5. **Joash**: son of Ahaziah; became Jehoash, King of Judah
6. **Jehosheba**: high priest's wife who rescued Joash
7. **Jehoiada**: high priest that protected Joash from Athaliah

MEMORY VERSE

PSALM 1

Blessed is the man that walketh not in the counsel of the ungodly, nor standeth in the way of sinners, nor sitteth in the seat of the scornful.

But his delight is in the law of the Lord; and in his law doth he meditate day and night.

And he shall be like a tree planted by the rivers of water, that bringeth forth his fruit in his season; his leaf also shall not wither; and whatsoever he doeth shall prosper.

The ungodly are not so; but are like the chaff which the wind driveth away. Therefore the ungodly shall not stand in the judgment, nor sinners in the congregation of the righteous.

For the Lord knoweth the way of the righteous: but the way of the ungodly shall perish.

- Ahab's son, Joram, is king of Israel. Ahab's grandson, Ahaziah, is king of Judah. The prophecy about the destruction of Ahab's posterity is about to be fulfilled.
- Elisha sends a prophet to Jehu in Gilead to anoint him king in Israel.
- The prophet anoints Jehu and tells him he will smite the house of Ahab.
- Jehu rides to Jezreel, where Joram is. He shoots an arrow through Joram, and he kills Ahaziah, who was also there with Joram.
- Jehu finds Jezebel, and he has her servants throw her down to the street from her window.
- Ahaziah's mother, Athaliah, put all the royal children to death so she could be queen of Judah. But one son, Joash, was rescued and hidden by Jehosheba, who was the wife of the high priest Jehoiada.
- After seven years, Jehoiada gathers the rulers and captains to make an oath to guard Joash during his coronation in the temple.
- Athaliah comes to the temple and cries, "Treason!" Jehoiada commands the captains to take her out, and she is slain.
- Jehoiada and the people promise the Lord to be His people. They broke down Baal's temple, altars, and they slew his priest.

COMPREHENSION QUESTIONS

1. Describe how Jehu was anointed king of Israel. __Elisha sent a prophet to take Jehu to__
an inner room, pour a vial of oil on his head, and say, "Thus says the Lord, I have
anointed you king over the people of the Lord, even over Israel ...." (p. 284)

2. What was Jehu's response to the horsemen when they asked him if he came in peace? What became of
the horsemen? _Jehu said, "What have you to do with peace? Get behind me." The_
horsemen did not return to the city. (p. 285)

3. Describe how the prophesy of Elijah regarding Ahab and Jezebel was fulfilled. ___After his anointing,__
Jehu set to cutting off Ahab's line. He killed Joram on the land of Naboth's vineyard and
slew Ahaziah as he escaped. On Jehu's order, Jezebel's servants threw her from the
window. Jehu trampled her to death on the street and had her buried. (p. 286)

4. What covenant did Jehoiada make with the rulers and captains concerning Joash? _They swore to_
divide into thirds guarding the house of the Lord and the person of the king. (p. 288)

5. What was the name that Joash reigned under?_____As king, he became Jehoash, which_
means "the Lord is strong." (p. 289)

BIG PICTURE OF THE BIBLE

Relate the following psalm passage to the events described in this lesson. Demonstrate how wonderful it is that though the ungodly plot and rebel, the righteousness of the Lord never changes.

• **Psalm 36:** What does the psalmist praise?

GEOGRAPHY

Review the locations of these places:

• Israel and Samaria
• Judea and Jerusalem
• Syria and Damascus
• Egypt
• Assyria and Nineveh

VOCABULARY AND EXPRESSIONS

1. **insignia**: a distinguishing mark or badge (Latin: *insignia*)
2. **coronation**: the occasion of crowning a monarch (from Latin *corona*, "crown")
3. **treason**: an attempt to undermine or overthrow a leader or government

ACTIVITIES

• pp. 284-285: Identify the two men in the picture. What question does the horseman have for the man in the chariot?
The horseman asks Jehu if he comes in peace.

• pp. 286-287: Who is Jehu pursuing in this picture? Where will he fall?
Jehu pursues Joram and slews him on the land where Naboth's vineyard once was.

• p. 289: Identify Joash, Jehoiada, Jehosheba, the captains, and Athaliah. What has just happened to Joash? What is about to happen to Athaliah?
Joash has just been crowned king of Judah, and Athaliah is being led out of the Temple to be killed for her treachery.

LESSON 18

BACKGROUND AND SUMMARY

As the failures of the Kings continued to increase, so also did the responsibilities of the Prophets. Despite their waywardness, God would not leave His people without a voice for spiritual renewal. A prophet was merely a mouthpiece for the Lord's will, sometimes foretelling, but mostly forthtelling. In this way, the prophets offer us some of the most unique and memorable articulations of both hope and warning we can find in the Bible. Let us consider these great gifts to us.

Amos: At a time in Israel's history when opulence and spiritual indifference were a social norm, Amos arose to speak for God and shake things up. Announcing God's imminent judgment on the people, Amos warned Israel that more importantly than the loss of land or goods, they would soon face a famine of God's word. His doomsday tone forecasted the horrors ahead.

Hosea: More than any other prophet, Hosea pictured the tragedy of covenant infidelity. With imagery and emotions he knew too well, Hosea described God's call of repentance in the language of a husband calling home his unfaithful bride. His promise of covenant restoration remains a timeless picture of God's enduring love for His people.

Isaiah: One of the greatest of all prophets, Isaiah presented both judgment and salvation, exile and restoration, and hope in the midst of darkness. Powerful in his theological articulations, Isaiah looked forward beyond Israel's present needs for deliverance to the greatest of God's future blessings, the Messiah. His description of the Messiah as a "Suffering Servant" remains the clearest picture of Jesus' life and sacrifice from the Old Testament. The poetic majesty of his writing and the depth of his message defies comparison.

LESSON 18: The Death of Elisha | Warnings From the Prophets
Golden Children's Bible: pp. 290-295 (II Kings 13, the Prophets)

FACTS TO KNOW

1. **Amos**: prophet who first predicted the fall of Hebrew nations because of their spiritual pride
2. **Hosea**: prophet who foretold disaster for Israel; held hope for God's mercy
3. **722 B.C.**: fall of Northern Kingdom to Assyria
4. **Isaiah**: one of the greatest prophets, preachers, statesmen, and political advisors in Judah for Amaziah, Uzziah, and Ahaz
5. **seraphim**: angels who sang and worshiped the Lord
6. **Ahaz**: king of Judah during the attack from Syria

MEMORY VERSE

> **ISAIAH 9:2, 6**
>
> *The people that walked in darkness have seen a great light. For unto us a child is born, unto us a son is given: and the government shall be upon his shoulder; and his name shall be called Wonderful, Counsellor, The mighty God, The everlasting Father, The Prince of Peace.*

1. Who does the prophecy in Genesis 3:14-15 speak about?
   Genesis 3:15 looks forward to a promised son that will conquer the seed of the serpent.

2. Who does Isaiah prophesy about?
   The birth of Israel's Messiah and King, Jesus Christ, God's own son.

3. What is the significance of each title?
   Each title tells us something about the Messiah.

   Wonderful Counselor:
   He will rule his kindgom with wisdom and authority.

   The Mighty God:
   He is a warrior who fights for His people.

   The Everlasting Father:
   His rule and covenant faithfulness will endure forever.

   The Prince of Peace:
   He will restore and make whole His people and His creation.

VOCABULARY AND EXPRESSIONS

1. **seraphim**: angelic creatures with six wings that ever worship God without looking directly at His glory
2. **respite**: rest or relief
3. **Immanuel**: "God is with us"

MEMORY WORK

All memory verses from Copybook and Christian Studies I are included in this book in the Appendix. Continue to review the Old Testament books (5-12-5-5-12).

1. What did Elisha predict about Jehoash before his death? Elisha prophesied that Jehoash would only strike Syria three times and Syria will not be completely destroyed. (p. 290)

2. What did Amos see as the sources of Israel's weakness? Amos spoke out against the life of luxury and spiritual indifference in Israel. The Israelites enjoyed the blessings without thanking the One who blesses. (p. 291)

3. What message did God send to Isaiah? Through an amazing vision, God sent Isaiah to the people of Israel to tell them they must change their ways. God told Isaiah that he was going to judge the people by removing His blessings and separating them from the land He had given them. (p. 293)

4. How did Ahaz and Judah survive the attack from Israel and the Syrians? God sent Assyria to answer Ahaz's request and to crush Israel and Syria. (p. 295)

5. When did the nation of Israel fall? Who conquered it? 722 B.C., to Assyria (p. 295)

6. What was an important role of prophets during this period in Salvation History? The ministry of the prophets was to interpret and demonstrate the actions of God in history. (p. 295)

GEOGRAPHY

1. Identify on your map the following countries and cities:
   - ☐ Israel
   - ☐ Judah
   - ☐ Syria
   - ☐ Assyria
   - ☐ Samaria
   - ☐ Jerusalem
   - ☐ Damascus
   - ☐ Nineveh

Lesson 18: The Death of Elisha I Warnings From the Prophets   71

ACTIVITIES

- Draw a picture from the lesson:

  1. Elisha prophesies to Jehoash from his deathbed about the Syrians.

  2. Isaiah sees the Lord enthroned in the Temple with angels attending and praising Him.

  3. Ahaz receives a sign from God through Isaiah's prophecy about the Messiah child.

- **Copybook Verse Review:** #35 in Appendix.

BIG PICTURE OF THE BIBLE

- **Isaiah 7:14; 9:2, 6; 11:1-5; 40:9-11**; and **52:13-53:12:** What does the prophet say about the coming Messiah?
- **Matthew 4:12-16:** Who fulfills what was written in Isaiah 9:2?
- **Ephesians 1:17-22:** How does Christ fulfill Isaiah 57:19?
- **Hebrews 1:1-2:** What is the revelation God has made?

PICTURING THE TRUTH

1. In this picture, it should be clear how dependent the king was upon the prophet, God's mouthpiece.

2. For this illustration, emphasize the same things that the Bible does, the majestic, supernatural imagery of God's throne room. Isaiah gets a glimpse of God's infinite holiness.

3. Amid the threat of military destruction, Ahaz receives a word of comfort from God through the prophet: "God is with us." Relate the significance of Immanuel as both a present and future reality of God's love.

GEOGRAPHY

Warnings from the Prophets:

- The country of **Assyria**, marked by the two darker shaded areas, would eventually destroy **Israel**.
- **Syria**, located north of **Israel**, attacked **Judah** when Ahaz was ruling. Syria's capital is **Damascus**.

LESSON 19

BACKGROUND AND SUMMARY

While Israel was the first of the Hebrew nations to receive the climax of God's judgment—Exile—Judah was to soon suffer the same consequence for her national apostasy. In the time leading up to the Fall of Jerusalem, two men surface from the wreckage of that nation to model faithfulness to God before the people. Let us examine the great contributions of their lives.

First, Josiah sticks in our memory because he was one of the few good kings in Judah's history. He was a good king because he restored the Book of the Law in the life of his people. This restoration was not merely lip service to religion, but a serious repentance modeled by the king himself (II Kings 22:11, 23:3). In this way, Josiah understood that God's expectations for the king meant leading the people through spiritual example. Though Josiah's reforms could not ultimately prevent the Exile, he was able to earn God's forbearance in his lifetime.

Second, when we think of a faithful prophet of God, Jeremiah should be the first on our list. Given the most difficult assignment of any of the prophets, Jeremiah's continual surrender to God's call in the midst of persecution from his people, the destruction of his home, and his own lamentation over Israel's failures stands in stark contrast to the perpetual infidelity of his countrymen. More than any other man of God, Jeremiah knew the full breadth of separation between the deep despair over the desolation of Jerusalem (Lamentation 3:1-18) and the bright hope of the coming Messiah (Jeremiah 23:5-8). Thus, Jeremiah remains one of the most complex voices in Scripture, because he looks straight at the suffering and offers the only hope there is for that pain, a Messiah that can establish a New Covenant.

In this way, the faithfulness of both Josiah and Jeremiah show us that no matter the conditions of life, God will always be pleased with those that take seriously the suffering that results from sin and put their trust in the Messiah that can bring deliverance, Jesus Christ.

FACTS TO KNOW

1. **Josiah**: good king of Judah; restored the Law and destroyed the idols of Baal
2. **Jeremiah**: prophet during the Fall of Jerusalem
3. **Pharaoh**: a king of Egypt
4. **Nineveh**: city of sin; Assyrian capital; fell to Babylon
5. **Chaldeans**: people of Babylon; formed a great empire
6. **Nebuchadnezzar**: king of Babylon; overthrew Jerusalem
7. **Zedekiah**: evil king of Jerusalem; disregarded Jeremiah
8. **586 B.C.**: Fall of Jerusalem, Babylonian captivity

MEMORY VERSE

> **JEREMIAH 31:31-33**
>
> *Behold, the days come, saith the Lord, that I will make a new covenant with the house of Israel and with the house of Judah: Not according to the covenant that I made with their fathers … which my covenant they break … but I will put my law in their inward parts, and write it in their hearts; and I will be their God, and they shall be my people.*

1. Why did God choose to make a "new covenant" with the people?
   The people could not keep the original covenant, because they kept forgetting the principles of God's Law.

2. Where was the law written originally? Where will it be written in the New Covenant?
   Initially, God put the law down on stone tablets for Moses and the people. In the New Covenant, however, God will impress His ways on the very hearts of the people.

3. In the last line, what is the goal of the New Covenant?
   The goal of the New Covenant is the restoration of the relationship between God and His people: He is faithful to them, and they faithfully bear His name.

VOCABULARY AND EXPRESSIONS

1. **"tore his clothes"**: physical expression of great emotion, usually grief or desperation

2. **"And he did that which was evil in the sight of the Lord."**: This phrase continually refers to the practice of idolatry. In line with many of the kings before him, Zedekiah also allowed pagan religions to exist in Judah.

COMPREHENSION QUESTIONS

1. What major event occurred during Josiah's reign in the 7th century B.C.? The Temple priests found the Book of the Law (Deuteronomy) and brought it to the king. (p. 296)

2. What does the Book of Deuteronomy contain? Deuteronomy contains the guidelines for Israel's worship and behavior, and it also outlines the covenant blessings and curses. (p. 296)

3. What did Josiah do that made him such a memorable and righteous king? He devoted himself to the Lord, emptied the temples of Baal and burned their ritual objects, and put down the idolatrous priests. (p. 297)

4. What did Jeremiah predict would happen to Israel? Why? Because they foresook the Lord, Israel would be conquered and exploited by a distant and foreign land. (p. 298)

5. How did Nebuchadnezzar destroy Jerusalem? Babylon seized all the treasure from the temple and palace and deported all the royal princes, warriors, and craftsmen, leaving only the poorest people. (p. 299)

6. How was Jeremiah punished for his warning? Who rescued him? He was thrown into a dungeon (the dry well of Machiah) until Zedekiah sent men to fetch him up. (p. 300)

7. How did Zedekiah respond to Jeremiah's warning? He ignored it. (pp. 302-303)

GEOGRAPHY

1. At this point in Israel's history, there is a changing of the guard among the superpowers in the Ancient Near East. The Assyrian empire shrinks to the growing might of Babylon. Point out the changing landscape of empires on the map. Also, relate the significance of the following areas and cities:

☐ Judah   ☐ Babylonia   ☐ Tigris River
☐ Jerusalem ☐ Assyria   ☐ Euphrates River
☐ Babylon   ☐ Egypt

BIG PICTURE OF THE BIBLE
- **Zephaniah 1:4-6:** What is the prophecy of Zephaniah?
- **Matthew 23:37-39:** How are Jesus and Jeremiah alike?
- **Hebrews 10:10-18:** How does Jesus fulfill Jeremiah's prophecy about a "New Covenant"?
- **Revelation 21:1-3:** What does St. John say the covenant community will be like? Observe the key phrase contained in both Jeremiah 31:33 and here.

MEMORY WORK
All memory verses from Copybook and Christian Studies I are included in this book in the Appendix. In this lesson, start reviewing Psalm 23. Continue to review the Old Testament books (5-12-5-5-12).

GEOGRAPHY
- The country of **Assyria**, which had conquered all the land from the **Persian Gulf to Egypt**, was itself conquered by **Babylonia**.
- The capital of **Babylonia** is **Babylon**.
- The capitals of both great superpowers were located near two rivers, the **Euphrates** and **Tigris**.

ACTIVITIES
- pp. 296-297: What are the elders of Judah and Jerusalem throwing into the fire?
  The elders are destroying the idols of the false gods that perverted Judah's worship.

- pp. 298-299: Describe what is taking place in this picture.
  The Chaldeans have taken the best people and possessions of Judah captive and are marching them to Babylon.

- pp. 302-303: Identify the men in this picture. What is happening here?
  Zedekiah's men are helping Jeremiah out of the dungeon pit in the prison court.

- **Copybook Verse Review:** Begin reviewing #30, Psalm 23, in Appendix.

LESSON 20

BACKGROUND AND SUMMARY

When the Exile and destruction of Judah finally took place, the people of Israel were utterly devastated. If they survived the horrific conditions of Nebuchadnezzar's siege of the city, then they would find themselves marching in shackles by caravan to Babylon, or left with the poorest inhabitants to put the pieces of their civilization back together. The modern reader struggles to imagine the level of physical hardship and desolation that took place, let alone Israel's sense of deep spiritual loss. The place of worship for Israel was almost as significant as the practice of worship. In this way, their habitation of the land remained a significant part of their covenant relationship with God. In other words, the Exile was not only a physical separation from Israel's home but also, in a very real sense, a spiritual separation from God. Consider the psalmist's depth of sorrow in this lesson's memory verse when he asks, "How shall we sing the Lord's song in a strange land?"

Despite the fact that Israel had left her God and was made to leave her land, the Lord had not completely abandoned His people. Even though the people could not fully worship their God in a foreign land, they still had the testimony of the prophets with them. Thus, Israel's hope came to rest upon the exilic prophets Daniel and Ezekiel.

LESSON 20: Jerusalem Is Destroyed | Songs of the Captives | Daniel
Golden Children's Bible: pp. 304-309 (II Kings 25, Psalm 137, Lam. 5, Daniel 1)

FACTS TO KNOW

1. **lamentation**: expression of grief and sadness
2. **Daniel**: Hebrew boy held captive in Babylon
3. **Shadrach, Meschach, and Abednego**: Hebrew exiles held captive with Daniel
4. **exiled**: removed from one's home country

MEMORY VERSE

> **PSALM 137:1-4**
>
> *By the rivers of Babylon, there we sat down, yea, we wept, when we remembered Zion. We hanged our harps upon the willows in the midst thereof.*
>
> *For there they that carried us away captive required of us a song; and they that wasted us required of us mirth, saying, Sing us one of the songs of Zion.*
>
> *How shall we sing the Lord's song in a strange land?*

1. What are willows?
   Willows are trees that grow by rivers; they are sad-looking trees because the branches hang down.

2. What is Zion?
   Jerusalem

3. What is the "strange land"?
   Babylon, the land of Judah's exile.

4. Who asked the children of Israel to sing, and why? What was their response?
   Their captors, the Babylonians, wanted to hear their songs. Their response was to ask how they could sing and be happy when they had been taken from their homes and were weeping.

5. Draw a picture that shows what the memory verse describes.

74   Lesson 20: Jerusalem Is Destroyed | Songs of the Captives | Daniel

---

VOCABULARY AND EXPRESSIONS

1. **vassal**: subordinate, under chief

2. **"raze it, raze it"**: demolish, smash, tear down

3. **"which was not the food of the children of Israel"**: In other words, Babylonian food did not fit the law of Moses' requirements for food (not kosher).

4. **"Happy shall he be that taketh and dasheth thy little ones against the stones."**: Unfortunately, the horrors of war have not changed much throughout the history of civilization even though the technology of war has. By this expression, the psalmist describes giving their captors the same inhuman treatment that they received in wartime.

COMPREHENSION QUESTIONS

1. Who destroyed Jerusalem in 586 B.C.? _____Nebuchadnezzer and the Chaldeans (p. 304)_____

2. Paraphrase the Lament of Jerusalem. __Because Judah angered the Lord, He has taken them__ from a place of great honor and blessing down to the lowest level of shame, sorrow, and despair. God has removed His special blessing from the people. (p. 305)

3. What do the children of Judah sing about in the Songs of the Captives? __They describe how God__ has rejected them, how they have been taken captive, exiled, and lost their families, inheritance, and homes. (p. 306)

4. Why were Daniel, Shadrach, Meshach, and Abednego raised in the palace? __They were the__ best of Judah's youths and were to be students of the Chaldeans. (p. 307)

5. Why did Daniel refuse the king's food? What was the result? __Daniel refused the food__ because it was unclean by Israel's law. He and the others ate only peas and beans for ten days, after which they were seen to be healthier than the children eating the meat and wine of the Chaldeans. (p. 308)

6. What gifts did God bestow upon the children? __The Lord blessed the boys with knowledge__ and skill ten times greater than the best of Babylon. (p. 309)

BIG PICTURE OF THE BIBLE

- **Deuteronomy 29:25-28:** What does Moses warn about in these verses? Then, in **Deuteronomy 30:1-10,** what is Moses' encouragement?

MEMORY WORK

All memory verses from Copybook and Christian Studies I are included in this book in the Appendix. In this lesson, continue reviewing Psalm 23 with the memorization of the Old Testament books (5-12-5-5-12).

GEOGRAPHY

Review all the locations using Review Map 3 in the Appendix, p. 136.

ACTIVITIES

- pp. 304-305: Identify the man being chased and the men pursuing him. What will become of this man?
  The Babylonian soldiers are pursuing Zedekiah, Judah's king, and will capture him on the plains of Jericho.

- p. 307: Identify the four boys in the picture by their Hebrew names.
  Daniel, Hananiah, Mishael, Azariah

- pp. 308-309: Describe the scene pictured here. What are the Babylonians trying to serve the boys? Why must they refuse to eat it?
  Daniel and the Hebrew boys are refusing the Babylonian food. Previously the servants of Nebuchadnezzar's house served pork and strong drink, which are both forbidden by the Law of Moses.

- **Copybook Verse Review:** Continue to review #30, Psalm 23, in Appendix.

REVIEW LESSON: Unit 4

INSTRUCTIONS

Use the Review Lesson to support mastery of the material presented in the previous five lessons. Drill the Facts to Know orally or have a Facts to Know Bee. Students may also write a description next to each fact on a separate piece of paper. Places to Know should be identified on the map at the end of this lesson. Students may work independently or with the teacher to complete the exercises. A test for this unit is included in the back of this book.

SALVATION HISTORY

Divided Kingdom Cont.
Elijah Commissions a Successor
God Judges the House of Ahab
Prophets Speak Warning
Israel and Syria Attack Judah
Assyria Conquers Israel
A Good King Restores the Law
Jerusalem Falls to Babylon

Dates to Know
586 B.C.
722 B.C.

People to Know
Elisha
Jehu
Joram
Ahaziah
Amos
Daniel
Gehazi
Hosea
Isaiah
Jehaiada
Ahaz
Josiah
Jeremiah
Nebuchadnezzar
Zedekiah
Athaliah
Jezebel
Joash
Naaman
Naboth

Places to Know
Assyria
Babylon
Babylonia
Damascus
Egypt
Euphrates River
Israel
Jerusalem
Jordan River
Judah
Nineveh
Samaria
Syria
Tigris River

Books of the O.T.
5-12-5-5-12

Genesis
Exodus
Leviticus
Numbers
Deuteronomy

Joshua
Judges
Ruth
I, II Samuel
I, II Kings
I, II Chronicles
Ezra
Nehemiah
Esther

Job
Psalms
Proverbs
Ecclesiastes
Song of Solomon

Isaiah
Jeremiah
Lamentations
Ezekiel
Daniel

Hosea
Joel
Amos
Obadiah
Jonah
Micah
Nahum
Habakkuk
Zephaniah
Haggai
Zechariah
Malachi

Words to Know/Vocabulary
sackcloth and ashes: worn during mourning
leper: one who suffers from skin disease; usually quarantined
Immanuel: name of the Messiah; means "God with us"
seraphim: angels worshiping the Lord
Pharaoh: a king of Egypt
lamentation: expression of grief and sadness
exiled: removed from one's home country
Zion: city of the most High God; Jerusalem

Give the corresponding word or phrase:

1. He was murdered by royalty for his vineyard. _Naboth_

2. She was the wicked, pagan wife of King Ahab of Israel. _Jezebel_

3. Elijah rode this to heaven so he never saw death. _chariot of fire_

4. He took the place of Elijah and saw his ascension to heaven. _Elisha_

5. the captain of Syria that was cured of leprosy by Elisha _Naaman_

6. Naaman washed himself clean of leprosy in this river. _Jordan_

7. He was the selfish servant of Elisha that got leprosy. _Gehazi_

8. This king set to punishing Ahab's family line. _Jehu_

9. She was queen of Judah for seven years after killing her family rivals. _Athaliah_

10. He was the king of Judah that was hidden in the Temple as a child. _Joash_

11. the Temple priest that protected the child king Joash _Jehoiada_

12. the names for the Messiah child _Wonderful, Counsellor, Mighty God, Everlasting Father, and Prince of Peace_

13. the first prophet to foretell the fall of Israel and Judah _Amos_

14. prophet of Israel that held out hope for God's mercy _Hosea_

15. The fall of the Northern kingdom happened in _722 B.C._

16. This nation conquered Israel. _Assyria_

17. greatest prophet, preacher, statesman, and advisor of Judah _Isaiah_

18. The seraphim sang this in Isaiah's vision. _"Holy, Holy, Holy is the Lord of hosts"_

19. the king who received a sign from Isaiah about the coming Messiah _Ahaz_

20. He was the Messiah child born to a virgin. _Jesus Christ_

21. the good king who reformed Judah according to the Book of the Law _Josiah_

22. He prophesied in Judah during the Fall of Jerusalem. _Jeremiah_

23. This nation took the best people and possessions of Jerusalem captive. _Babylon_

24. Instead of stone tablets, the New Covenant will be written on people's _hearts_

25. The Fall of Jerusalem happened in _586 B.C._

OLD TESTAMENT DRILL QUESTIONS

The drill questions from Christian Studies I have been compiled in the Appendix. These questions will be used in each of the subsequent study guides for Christian Studies. Continue reviewing these as the year progresses.

REVIEW LESSON: Unit 4

TIMELINE REVIEW

Review the Big Picture of the Bible, so students understand the major periods (i.e., Creation, Patriarchs, Exodus, etc.). When they understand the periods, continue filling in the Full Timeline in the Appendix and populate each period with the important people. In this way, they will associate each person with the right events. (Example: Moses = Exodus)

Match up the Words to Know:

E   1. sackcloth and ashes

H   2. leper

B   3. Immanuel

A   4. seraphim

G   5. Pharaoh

C   6. lamentation

D   7. exiled

F   8. Zion

A. worshiping God in heaven

B. "God with us"

C. expression of sadness

D. removed from one's home

E. worn during mourning

F. another name for Jerusalem

G. a king of Egypt

H. quarantined with skin disease

SALVATION HISTORY TIMELINE

Put these events in the correct order.

Divided Kingdom Continued

3   Prophets Speak Warning

1   Elijah Commissions a Successor

6   A Good King Restores the Law

4   Israel and Syria Attack Judah

7   Jerusalem Falls to Babylon

5   Assyria Conquers Israel

2   God Judges the House of Ahab

COMPREHENSION QUESTIONS

Answer these comprehension questions from the lesson.

1. What did Elisha ask of Elijah before he departed? Elisha requested a double portion of Elijah's spirit. (p. 280)

2. Describe how Elijah's prophecy regarding Ahab and Jezebel was fulfilled. After his anointing, Jehu set to cutting off Ahab's line. He killed Joram on the land of Naboth's vineyard and slew Ahaziah as he escaped. On Jehu's order, Jezebel's servants threw her from the window. Jehu trampled her to death on the street and had her buried. (p. 286)

3. What did Amos see as the cause of Israel's weakness? Amos spoke out against the life of luxury and spiritual indifference in Israel. The Israelites enjoyed the blessings without thanking the One who blesses. (p. 291)

4. What did Josiah do that made him such a memorable and righteous king? He devoted himself to the Lord, emptied the temples of Baal and burned their ritual objects, and put down the idolatrous priests. (p. 297)

5. Why did Daniel refuse the king's food? What was the result? Daniel refused the food because it was unclean by Israel's law. He and the others ate only peas and beans for ten days, after which they were seen to be healthier than the children eating the meat and wine of the Chaldeans. (p. 308)

REVIEW LESSON: Unit 4

MEMORY VERSES

To recite memory verses, give the first few words and let students complete the verse orally. Students should write the verse from memory or copy it from the lesson.

Check each box if you can recite the Scripture verse from memory. Write each from memory or teacher dictation. Be accurate.

☐ II Kings 2:11 ___ There appeared a chariot of fire and horses of fire, and Elijah went up by a whirlwind into heaven. _____

☐ Psalm 1 ___ Blessed is the man that walketh not in the counsel of the ungodly, nor standeth in the way of sinners, nor sitteth in the seat of the scornful. But his delight is in the law of the Lord; and in his law doth he meditate day and night. And he shall be like a tree planted by the rivers of water, that bringeth forth his fruit in his season; his leaf also shall not wither; and whatsoever he doeth shall prosper. The ungodly are not so; but are like the chaff which the wind driveth away. Therefore the ungodly shall not stand in the judgment, nor sinners in the congregation of the righteous. For the Lord knoweth the way of the righteous: but the way of the ungodly shall perish. _____

☐ Isaiah 9:2, 6 ___ The people that walked in darkness have seen a great light. For unto us a child is born, unto us a son is given: and the government shall be upon his shoulder; and his name shall be called Wonderful, Counsellor, The mighty God, The everlasting Father, The Prince of Peace. _____

☐ Jeremiah 31:31-33 ___ Behold, the days come, saith the Lord, that I will make a new covenant with the house of Israel and with the house of Judah: Not according to the covenant that I made with their fathers … which my covenant they break … but I will put my law in their inward parts, and write it in their hearts; and I will be their God, and they shall be my people. _____

☐ Psalm 137:1-4 ___ By the rivers of Babylon, there we sat down, yea, we wept, when we remembered Zion. We hanged our harps upon the willows in the midst thereof. For there they that carried us away captive required of us a song; and they that wasted us required of us mirth, saying, Sing us one of the songs of Zion. How shall we sing the Lord's song in a strange land? _____

LESSON 19: Josiah | The Fall of Jerusalem | Jeremiah
Golden Children's Bible: pp. 296-303 (II Kings 22-24, Jeremiah 5, 37-38)

Put the following in order on the timeline below.

1. **Dates**: Time Begins, The Fall of Jerusalem (586 B.C.), Reign of David (1000 B.C.), The Call of Abraham (2000 B.C.), The Fall of Israel (722 B.C.), Exodus (1400 B.C.), Divided Kingdom (931 B.C.)

2. **Periods**: Judges, Patriarchs, United Kingdom, Exodus, Prehistory, Divided Kingdom, Conquest

3. **Events**: The Fall of Jericho, The Creation, God's Covenant with David, The Fall of Jerusalem, Ten Commandments, Elijah Defeats Prophets of Baal, The Child of Promise

4. **People**: David, Sarah, Moses, Solomon, Adam, Josiah, Abraham, Isaiah, Gideon, Joshua

Date	Events	Period	People
Time Begins	The Creation	Prehistory	Adam
2000 B.C.		Patriarchs	Abraham and Sarah
	The Child of Promise		
1400 B.C.		Exodus	Moses
	Ten Commandments		
		Conquest	Joshua
	The Fall of Jericho		
		Judges	
			Gideon
1000 B.C.		United Kingdom	David
	God's Covenant with David		
			Solomon
931 B.C.		Divided Kingdom	
	Elijah Defeats Baal		
722 B.C.			
			Isaiah
			Josiah
586 B.C.	The Fall of Jerusalem		

MORE TIMELINE REVIEW

We cannot overstate the importance of each student truly understanding the Old Testament chronology. The Bible is God's story and, as a story, sequence is very important!

We have included here a big picture practice timeline. Continue to help students identify the storyline based on the dates, periods, events, and important people.

REVIEW LESSON: Unit 4

BOOKS OF THE OLD TESTAMENT

The Books of the Law

1. Genesis
2. Exodus
3. Leviticus
4. Numbers
5. Deuteronomy

The Books of History

1. Joshua
2. Judges
3. Ruth
4. I Samuel
5. II Samuel
6. I Kings
7. II Kings
8. I Chronicles
9. II Chronicles
10. Ezra
11. Nehemiah
12. Esther

The Books of Wisdom

1. Job
2. Psalms
3. Proverbs
4. Ecclesiastes
5. Song of Solomon

The Books of the Major Prophets

1. Isaiah
2. Jeremiah
3. Lamentations
4. Ezekiel
5. Daniel

The Books of the Minor Prophets

1. Hosea
2. Joel
3. Amos
4. Obadiah
5. Jonah
6. Micah
7. Nahum
8. Habakkuk
9. Zephaniah
10. Haggai
11. Zechariah
12. Malachi

MAP WORK

Places to Know

☐ Assyria
☐ Babylon
☐ Babylonia
☐ Damascus
☐ Egypt

☐ Euphrates River
☐ Israel
☐ Jerusalem
☐ Judah
☐ Nineveh

☐ Samaria
☐ Syria
☐ Tigris River

We recommend that the student first locate and highlight the place to know on the labeled map, then use the blank map to practice identifying the places.

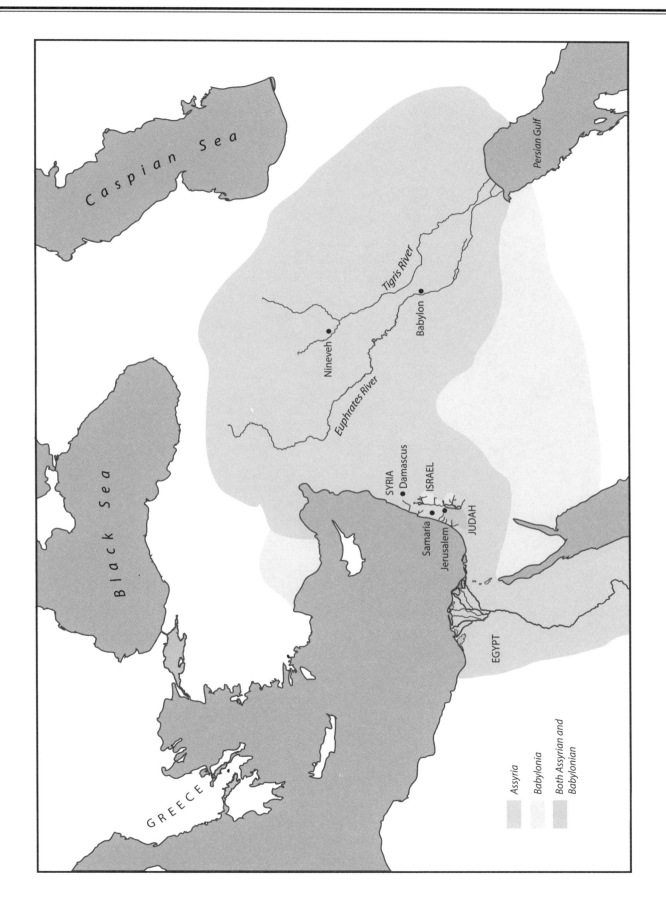

Caspian Sea

Persian Gulf

Tigris River

Babylon

Nineveh

Euphrates River

Black Sea

SYRIA
Damascus
ISRAEL
JUDAH
Samaria
Jerusalem

EGYPT

GREECE

Assyria

Babylonia

Both Assyrian and
Babylonian

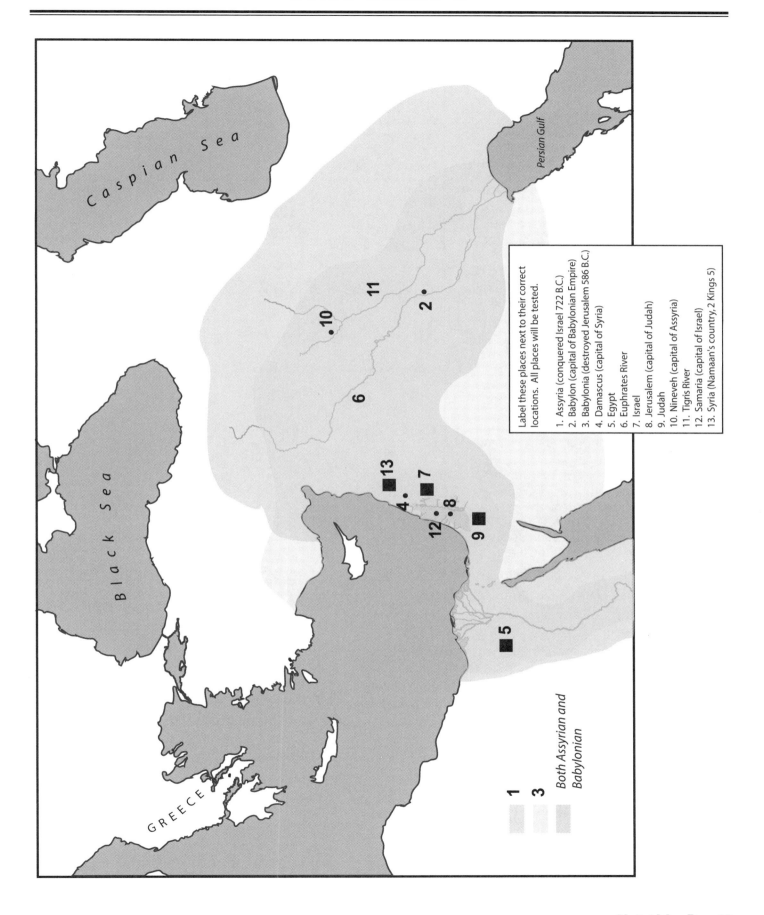

Label these places next to their correct locations. All places will be tested.

1. Assyria (conquered Israel 722 B.C.)
2. Babylon (capital of Babylonian Empire)
3. Babylonia (destroyed Jerusalem 586 B.C.)
4. Damascus (capital of Syria)
5. Egypt
6. Euphrates River
7. Israel
8. Jerusalem (capital of Judah)
9. Judah
10. Nineveh (capital of Assyria)
11. Tigris River
12. Samaria (capital of Israel)
13. Syria (Namaan's country, 2 Kings 5)

Caspian Sea

Persian Gulf

Black Sea

GREECE

1

3

Both Assyrian and Babylonian

LESSON 21

BACKGROUND AND SUMMARY

During the Exile, the prophets rose to a place of supreme importance because, unlike the priests and kings, their ministry was not limited by geography. Through the exilic prophets, God would reveal Himself not only to Israel, but also the world. Thus, the category of those who can enter God's covenant community began to widen. The first stage of this widening began with God making known His name and His power to the pagan kings. Pay careful attention to the way in which the pagan kings respond to the miraculous demonstrations of God's protection for His prophets (for example, see Daniel 3:28-29). In this, God used Daniel in mighty ways.

Daniel and his Hebrew friends were selected as the elite youths of Israel. Though they were enlisted to learn the wisdom of Babylon, they would soon prove to have a superior wisdom from God. While in exile, they demonstrated an amazing faithfulness to God. Even though they could not help the fact that they were prisoners of Babylon, Daniel and his friends made the commitment to seize control of each opportunity to please the Lord with their personal holiness. They did not allow the circumstances of life to dictate their loyalty to God. We should each apply that same sort of resolve in our lives.

The story of this lesson is as follows:

- Nebuchadnezzar builds a statue of gold and commands everyone to worship it or be put in a furnace.
- Shadrach, Meshach, and Abednego refuse, they are accused, and the king puts them in the furnace.
- Some of the king's men were killed by the furnace's heat, but the three Jews were unhurt, and a fourth man was in the fire with them.
- The king blesses their God and decrees death to anyone who speaks against him. He promotes them.
- While Belshazzar holds a feast with vessels from God's temple, writing appears on the wall.
- The king's wise men cannot interpret it, so Daniel is called.
- Daniel tells the prophecy: God has judged Belshazzar for his pride and will take the kingdom from him and give it to the Medes and Persians.

LESSON 21: The Statue of Gold | The Writing on the Wall
Golden Children's Bible: pp. 310-317 (Daniel 3, 5)

FACTS TO KNOW

1. **Nebuchadnezzar**: king of Babylon; built statue of gold
2. **Belshazzar**: son of Nebuchadnezzar; ruled after his father
3. **provinces**: divisions of a region
4. **Shadrach, Meshach, and Abednego**: Hebrew children unharmed by the fires
5. **Expression to Remember**: "Writing on the Wall"
6. **edict**: proclamation from a king

MEMORY VERSE

> **DANIEL 5:25-28**
>
> *And this was the writing that was written, MENE, MENE, TEKEL, UPHARSIN. This is the interpretation of the thing: MENE; God hath numbered thy kingdom, and finished it. TEKEL; Thou art weighed in the balances, and art found wanting. PERES; Thy kingdom is divided and given to the Medes and Persians.*

1. Where did the hand of God write on the wall?
   God wrote on the wall in the palace of the Babylonian king Belshazzar.

2. Who was the interpreter?
   Daniel was summoned to give an interpretation.

3. What does it mean to be "weighed in the balances" and "found wanting"?
   These expressions mean to be judged and determined to be inadequate.

VOCABULARY AND EXPRESSIONS

1. **"like the Son of God"**: The fourth figure in the furnace was what Nebuchadnezzar believed to be an angelic being (Daniel 3:28). Some Bible scholars think that this may be a pre-incarnational appearance of Jesus Christ.

2. **"Writing on the Wall"**: This expression describes an omen of someone's unpleasant destiny.

3. **"you have not kept your heart simple"**: meaning you have not humbled yourself before God

COMPREHENSION QUESTIONS

1. Describe the statue Nebuchadnezzar built. ___The statue was made of gold and stood 90 feet___ high and 9 feet wide. (p. 310)

2. What threat did the king give his people regarding the statue? ___The king decided that those who___ did not fall down and worship the statue would be cast into a fiery furnace. (pp. 310-311)

3. Why were the Jewish children thrown into a fiery furnace? ___They would not bow to the statue___ and worship the Babylonian gods. (p. 312)

4. What happened to the children while in the furnace? What happened to the men who prepared the furnace? The men who led them were killed by the flames, but the children were unharmed and were accompanied in the furnace by one who looked like the Son of God. (p. 312)

5. What came about as a result of God's miracle and the children's devotion? _____ Nebuchadnezzer decreed that no one should speak against the God of Shadrach, Meshach, and Abednego, who were promoted to high offices of Babylon. (p. 313)

6. Who was called to read the writing on the wall? What did it say? ___Daniel was called to read the___ writing. It said "Mene Mene Tekel Upharsin," which was interpreted that the kingdom was found lacking, was finished, and would be divided. (p. 317)

7. How was Daniel rewarded? ___Daniel was given a position of honor in the kingdom and he___ was clothed in scarlet, given a chain of gold, and made third ruler in the kingdom. (p. 317)

BIG PICTURE OF THE BIBLE

- **Deuteronomy 5:6-10:** How does Moses restate the first two decrees of the Ten Commandments? Relate these foundational points of the Law of Moses to the story of Shadrach, Meshach, and Abednego.

MEMORY WORK

All memory verses from Copybook and Christian Studies I are included in this book in the Appendix. Continue reviewing Psalm 23. With the memorization of the Old Testament books (5-12-5-5-12), keep reviewing the twelve books of the Minor Prophets.

ACTIVITIES

- pp. 310-311: Describe the scene in Dura pictured here. What does the idol resemble? What are the people doing?
  The Babylonians have gathered on the plain to worship an idol resembling a man or maybe a king.

- pp. 312-313: Identify the Hebrew youths. What do their expressions tell you?
  Shadrach, Meshach, and Abednego appear in the fire, but do not feel the effects of it; they are not burned, nor do they feel pain.

- pp. 314-315: Identify Belshazzar. What has interrupted his party? Describe the expressions of the people.
  The king and his party guests have been startled and even frightened by the very hand of God writing a cryptic message upon the wall.

- pp. 316-317: Who is the prophet that is discerning the message for the king? Who took Belshazzar's kingdom that night?
  Daniel interprets the message; Darius the Mede took the kingdom.

- **Copybook Verse Review:** Continue to review #30, Psalm 23, in Appendix.

LESSON 22

BACKGROUND AND SUMMARY

God used Daniel's successful career as a political advisor to the overlords of the Near Eastern empires to showcase His global interests. As God's universal plan of redemption became clearer in the message of the prophets, His people began to understand that Yahweh would not only be the Lord of Israel, but also the Lord over all peoples. In the meantime, however, God was pleased to protect and honor Daniel's ministry as a prophet to the nations and the exilic people of Israel. Again, observe how the pagan king appropriately responds to the divine protection by which Daniel was saved from the lions' den (Daniel 6:20-28). Consider how many pagan kings marvelled at the Lord because of Daniel's faithfulness: Nebuchadnezzar, Belshazzar, Darius, and Cyrus.

In addition to the prophetic ministry of Daniel, the exilic priest Ezekiel ministered the word of the Lord to the children of Israel in Babylon. Ezekiel preached for a complete repentance and a comprehensive restoration for Israel (Ezekiel 33:11 and 37:12). His words about Israel's restoration looked beyond a mere return to the land. Instead, the focus of Israel's renewal became the heart of the individuals that made up the community of God's people. Therefore, salvation became more than a physical deliverance from outside oppressors, but a spiritual deliverance from one's own inability to fulfill the Law of Moses. Along these lines, consider Ezekiel's announcement that God will remove the heart of stone from His people and replace it with a new, pure heart of flesh (Ezekiel 36:22-29). What kind of heart do we each have, hardened stone or renewed purity?

The story of this lesson is as follows:

- Darius makes Daniel the first of three presidents over the kingdom. The other presidents and princes plot to undermine Daniel.
- They convince Darius to decree a law prohibiting prayer to any god but the king for 30 days under threat of death in the lions' den.
- Daniel keeps praying to God, and so he is accused by the plotters. Although Darius tries to save him, at last he gives in to the officials and puts Daniel in the lions' den.
- The next day the king finds Daniel unhurt, because God's angel had shut the lions' mouths. Daniel's accusers are given to the lions. Darius praises God and commands all in the kingdom to tremble before Him.
- Ezekiel, a Jewish prophet in Babylon, heard God's word and saw visions from the Lord about the mercy and grace He would show Israel in times to come.

FACTS TO KNOW

1. **Medes and Persians**: the next great empire of the Ancient Near East; consumed Babylon
2. **Darius the Mede**: king of the Medes and Persians; took over Belshazzar's empire
3. **Cyrus the Persian**: next king of Medes and Persians
4. **Ezekiel**: prophet and priest who lived in Babylon
5. **Isaiah**: prophesied both judgment and return from exile

MEMORY VERSE

DANIEL 6:23

So Daniel was taken up out of the den, and no manner of hurt was found upon him, because he believed in his God.

---

1. How had God protected Daniel from the lions?
   God sent angels to shut the mouths of the hungry lions.

2. Why did God protect Daniel from the lions?
   God saved Daniel because Daniel trusted both the Lord's goodness to save and His power to protect.

COMPREHENSION QUESTIONS

1. Why did Darius make a law about only worshiping the king? ___The evil advisors of Darius___ wanted to get rid of Daniel and encouraged the king to outlaw all other religions. (p. 318)

2. Why was Daniel thrown into a lions' den? ___Despite the king's new law, Daniel continued to___ show his faith in Babylon and pray to the living God of Israel. (p. 319)

3. How did King Darius feel about Daniel's punishment? What was his hope? ___Darius was___ displeased with himself but he hoped that Daniel's God would save him. (p. 319)

4. What happened to Daniel in the lions' den? What happened to Daniel's accusers? _____ Daniel was unharmed because God sent angels to shut the lions' mouths, but the evil advisors did not have such divine protection. (pp. 320-321)

5. What proclamation did Darius make after Daniel's miracle? ___Darius decreed that all should___ respect the God of Daniel, the living God who rescues and saves. (p. 321)

6. The prophets of the exile held out both warning and hope for the people. What was the warning, and what was their hope? ___The prophets warned the people of God's justice in punishing their___ evil ways. They also extended a word of hope that God would soon bring about a return to Jerusalem and an even greater spiritual restoration. (pp. 322-323)

HISTORY

1. Memorize the three kings of Persia:
   - ☐ Cyrus
   - ☐ Darius (not the Mede)
   - ☐ Artaxerxes

Lesson 22: Daniel in the Lions' Den |Prophets of the Exile **89**

BIG PICTURE OF THE BIBLE

- **Ezekiel 36:22-29:** What do Ezekiel's words about the new heart closely resemble?
- **Ezekiel 37:24-28:** What are Ezekiel's hopes concerning the Davidic Messiah?
- **II Corinthians 5:17:** See St. Paul's announcement of Christ making his followers into "new creatures." His concept of a person as a new creation in Christ echoes Ezekiel and Jeremiah's prophecy about God giving His people a "new heart."
- **Hebrews 9:13-15:** How does this passage pick up on the "sprinkling hearts clean" from Ezekiel 36:25?

MEMORY WORK

All memory verses from Copybook and Christian Studies I are included in this book in the Appendix. Start reviewing Psalm 100:1-3.

PICTURING THE TRUTH

For this illustration, it is important to emphasize both Daniel's complete confidence in his God and Darius's profound response of elation and praise to Daniel's God. Draw a picture that shows Daniel's safe release from the lions' den.

ACTIVITIES

- pp. 318-319: Identify the men pictured here. What has been brought before the king?
  The wicked advisors have brought King Darius an edict to sign that will outlaw any religion that does not worship the king.

- pp. 320-321: What has happened to Daniel? Who is looking down on him?
  Daniel has been preserved from the attack of the lions, and Darius has come to see him saved by his God.

- pp. 322-323: Reread Isaiah's prophecy on p. 323. Why is the picture of shepherds tending their sheep a proper illustration for this lesson?
  Isaiah said that the Lord would care for and shepherd tenderly the flock of his people in the day of their return from exile.

- **Copybook Verse Review:** Begin to review #31, Psalm 100:1-3, in Appendix.

LESSON 23

BACKGROUND AND SUMMARY

In line with the word of the prophets, God impressed upon the king's heart to initiate the return of Israel to the land. When the people began arriving home, they found their land and culture in ruin. Amid the restoration efforts, there arose two central figures to lead the people.

First, Ezra pioneered religious and spiritual reform for the returning exiles. The people had been banished from the land for their inability to keep themselves committed to Yahweh. Thus, Ezra led the people to hear the words of the Law (Nehemiah 8:1-3). His reading was, for many, the first time they heard what their God expected of them. The people were captivated by the Word, and the public proclamation of Scripture brought about repentance and worship in the congregation (Nehemiah 9). Thus, we should note the power of God's Word to restore spiritual life to those who have lost hope and direction.

Secondly, Nehemiah provided godly leadership to rebuild the city walls. Taking the vision God had given him, Nehemiah bravely oversaw the building in the midst of opposition from within and without the people. Nehemiah's great legacy as a leader was his simple trust in God. Leading by example, he took God's promises to heart and faithfully served the mission, acknowledging his dependence on God's help along the way. He remains for us a model of humble service to God.

Despite the heroic contributions of Ezra and Nehemiah, one glaring problem stands out. Israel was back in the land, but Zerubbabel's Temple was miniature in comparison to Solomon's (Ezra 3:12) and the Davidic king was replaced with a subservient governor. What about the great, pervasive restoration the prophets spoke about?

The story of this lesson is as follows:

- The Lord stirs Cyrus to send God's people back to Jerusalem to rebuild the Temple. The chiefs of Judah and Benjamin and the priests and Levites are given treasures and items from the old Temple.
- After two years in Jerusalem, the people start rebuilding the Temple. They encounter some opposition, but Darius ends it.
- After some years, Nehemiah is stirred to go help rebuild the walls of Jerusalem. He asks King Artaxerxes for permission.

LESSON 23: The Return to Jerusalem
Golden Children's Bible: pp. 324-331 (Ezra 1-6, Nehemiah 1-6)

FACTS TO KNOW

1. **Cyrus**: king of Persia; charged the reconstruction of the Temple
2. **536 B.C.**: first exiles return to Jerusalem
3. **Darius**: king of Persia; decreed protection for those rebuilding the Temple
4. **Artaxerxes**: king of Persia; released Ezra and sent Nehemiah to rebuild the city walls
5. **Ezra**: scribe and priest who led the reform when the people returned
6. **Nehemiah**: royal cupbearer; oversaw the rebuilding of Jerusalem's city walls

MEMORY VERSE

> **EZRA 7:27**
>
> *Blessed be the Lord God of our fathers, which hath put such a thing as this in the king's heart, to beautify the house of the Lord which is in Jerusalem.*

1. Who is the king that Ezra has written about with praise?
   Ezra thanked God for compelling the heart of Artaxerxes to send the people back to rebuild the Temple.

2. What did the king do to "beautify the house of the Lord"?
   The king gave the money that the Hebrews needed to rebuild and restore the Temple.

VOCABULARY AND EXPRESSIONS

1. **adversaries**: opponents or enemies (from Latin *adversus*, "turned against")

2. **jeered**: taunted or teased

1. According to the proclamation, who was to build a house at Jerusalem? Who had foreseen this return and announced the prophecy? __Cyrus would rebuild the Temple. Jeremiah had foretold the__ __return in Jeremiah 29:10. (p. 324)__

2. Describe the return of the people out of captivity and their work on the house of the Lord. __Two years after their return, the exiles began work on the Temple amid the opposition__ __of local enemies throughout the reign of Cyrus. (p. 326)__

3. When was the house of the Lord finished? __The house was finished in the sixth year of the__ __reign of Darius. (p. 327)__

4. When visitors from Judah arrived in Persia, why was Nehemiah so sad? __Hearing of the pitiful__ __condition of those who had remained in Jerusalem, Nehemiah grieved over the__ __misfortune of his people. (p. 328)__

5. What did Nehemiah's two letters from the king promise? __Artaxerxes gave him both a letter__ __promising safety through Judah and a letter to Asaph, the keeper of the king's forest,__ __allowing Nehemiah to demand timber. (p. 329)__

6. How did Nehemiah organize the work? How long did it take for the wall to be finished? __Nehemiah enlisted the help of all the people and split them into work parties based__ __upon their families and clans. The work totaled 52 days. (p. 331)__

GEOGRAPHY

1. Follow the exiles' return journey to Jerusalem from these locations in Babylonia:
   - ☐ Babylon
   - ☐ Nippur
   - ☐ Susa

Lesson 23: The Return to Jerusalem   **91**

BIG PICTURE OF THE BIBLE

- **Jeremiah 29:10:** What does God promise to do for His people?
- **Ezra 3:8-13** and **6:13-18:** See the account of the Temple's restoration and dedication.
- **Nehemiah 8:1-3:** Observe the dramatic scene where Ezra reads the Law of Moses to the people.
- Revisit Jesus' claims to be a better Temple, found in **Matthew 12:6** and **John 2:19**.

GEOGRAPHY

Babylon, Nippur, and Susa were important cities of ancient Babylonia and Persia. The exiles would have returned from many cities, including these three:

- **Babylon** was the first capital city of the Persian Empire.
- **Nippur** was a "holy city" for the Persian gods.
- After Cyrus, the capital was moved to **Susa**.

ACTIVITIES

- pp. 324-325: Identify those pictured here. Why are the men carrying vessels of silver and gold?
  Cyrus gave the Jews their sacred objects so they might return them to the Temple when it was rebuilt.

- pp. 326-327: Describe the picture in your own words. What is taking place?
  The exiles who have returned have started restoring the Temple.

- pp. 328-329: Who is the man in this picture? What is the city in the background? Describe the state of the city's fortifications.
  Nehemiah surveys the status of Jerusalem's walls and finds them in very poor condition.

- pp. 330-331: Who is at work on the walls?
  Here, Nehemiah has gained the help of all the people; men and women, rich and poor, young and old.

- **Copybook Verse Review:** Continue to review #31, Psalm 100:1-3, in Appendix.

LESSON 24

BACKGROUND AND SUMMARY

The Psalms remain one of the most significant contributions to our canon of Scripture and the key source for teaching us about prayer and worship. Compiled over a millennia spanning from the Exodus to the return from Exile, these sacred songs reveal God's inspired instruction on how He is to be worshiped and adored. More than merely a worship how-to text, Psalms leads us by providing both the form and content of worship. The beautiful poetic verses teach us how to shape and form our praise to God, and at the same time, the message and spirit of the verses lead us in ways to think and feel toward God. The vibrant, rich worship of both the Old and New Testaments thrives on that sort of wholistic worship. Let us summarize briefly the great value of Psalms for us today.

First, Psalms puts the contemporary worshiper in touch with ancient realities. So many times "modern" Christians struggle to experience God in worship because they are only concerned with what they are presently a part of, the here and now. Well, the prayers and praises of Psalms are rooted in the historical consciousness of the Bible. God has acted in history, and that story is of supreme importance. In this way, Psalms helps to change our perspective toward viewing ourselves as a part of Salvation History.

Second, Psalms communicates in the broadest spectrum of emotions. We cannot experience a feeling of joy or despair today that the psalmist has not used to pen a prayer or praise to God. Thus, when we read and relate to these verses, we experience a connection with saints like David, Moses, and Ezra.

Third, Psalms is a holy standard for worship. Left to our own devices, we could produce some very unhealthy worship practices. Without God's help, we turn the focus of worship inward on ourselves. To this deficiency, we go to the rich text of Psalms that gives us inspired thoughts to think, pray, and sing. Probably of greatest value, Psalms leads us in "self-forgetful" worship and directs our attention back to the Lord.

VOCABULARY AND EXPRESSIONS

1. "When the Lord **turned again** the captivity of Zion": returned, brought back

2. **Zion**: the holy city of God; heavenly Jerusalem; the spiritual dwelling of the people of God

3. **heathen**: nations, gentiles, non-Jews

LESSON 24: Psalms of Joy
Golden Children's Bible: pp. 332-333 (Psalm 23, 24, 100, 126)

FACTS TO KNOW

Review the Psalms you have learned:

☐ Psalm 1   ☐ Psalm 23   ☐ Psalm 121
☐ Psalm 19:1-3   ☐ Psalm 100   ☐ Psalm 137:1-4

MEMORY VERSE

> **PSALM 122:1, 2, 6**
>
> *I was glad when they said unto me, Let us go into the house of the Lord.*
> *Our feet shall stand within thy gates, O Jerusalem.*
> *Pray for the peace of Jerusalem: they shall prosper that love thee.*

1. What is "the house of the Lord"?
   The Temple is the house of the Lord.

2. Provide some reasons why Jerusalem is such an important place for the psalmist.
   The Ark of the Covenant resides in the Temple in Jerusalem. Jerusalem was the capital of the Davidic kingdom. For Israel, Jerusalem will always be the holy city.

3. Has Jerusalem remained at peace? Why or why not?
   No, Jerusalem has not been at peace. In 70 A.D., the Romans destroyed the city and dispersed the Jews. Throughout the Middle Ages, Muslims controlled the area. Even today, Jerusalem is the source of much conflict.

COMPREHENSION QUESTIONS

1. What is a psalm? _A psalm is a ritual song for biblical worship. (p. 332)_

2. How were the Psalms used in biblical times and now even today? _They have been used as central parts of religious services both in biblical times and in synagogues and churches today. (p. 332)_

3. What is the message of each of the Psalms 23, 24, 100, 126? _Psalm 23 is a song of comfort and peace. Psalm 24 is a declaration of God's glory. Psalm 100 is a call to worship. Psalm 126 celebrates the historical reality of the return from exile. (*This is a great opportunity for students to reflect back on the historical events leading up to this point. Students should read the Psalms and incorporate all they have learned to answer this question.)_

4. What does each Psalm (23, 24, 100, 126) uniquely teach about God's nature or character? _Psalm 23 describes the tenderness of God's love. Psalm 24 affirms boldly both the holiness and might of the Lord. Psalm 100 praises God as the merciful, everlasting Lord of Creation and His people. Psalm 126 announces the jubilant salvation God brings._

5. Why was the 126th Psalm written? _It celebrates the homecoming of the Jews. (p. 332)_

BIG PICTURE OF THE BIBLE

• **John 10:11:** Read about Jesus' declaration of himself as the good shepherd.

PICTURING THE TRUTH

These illustrations should focus on the various imagery of the Psalms (i.e., a peaceful shepherd, a fortified city on a hill, a homeward caravan, etc.). Encourage the students to discuss virtues of peace, holiness, and joy displayed in these images. Unlike passages of biblical prose, the beauty of the Psalm poetry is found in the rich, imagery-laden language that provides particular pictures for universal spiritual truths. Use these images to communicate those powerful truths of God's character.

ACTIVITIES

• Draw your own pictures to go along with the Psalms featured in this lesson.
• p. 333: Identify the types of instruments shown in the picture.
• **Copybook Verse Review:** Continue to review #31, Psalm 100:1-3, in Appendix.

LESSON 25

BACKGROUND AND SUMMARY

As the period of the writings of the Old Testament ended, there was a growing tension between the fact that Israel had experienced only a partial restoration and the message of the prophets began to include a theme of salvation for all nations. There is no greater example of this unsettling tension in the Old Testament than what we find in the book of Jonah.

In its own unique way, the story of Jonah teaches us an astounding truth about God's mercy. Quite representative for Israel, Jonah's stubbornness about ministering God's word of warning to Assyria reveals the firm belief of some Jews that God could have no other special people than Israel. While Jonah's animosity toward Nineveh was quite justified—since Assyria's wickedness included horrible practices in war, prostitution, and witchcraft— it represented a fundamental misunderstanding of God's ways. The Lord was about to extend His mercy beyond Israel. Instead of judging the nations through Israel, God was using Israel to proclaim His salvation abroad. In this way, God's miraculous acts of saving Jonah and preserving him for the mission reveal His great determination to bring the nations to a knowledge and fear of their Creator.

FACTS TO KNOW

1. **Jonah**: prophet of God unwillingly sent to Nineveh after being swallowed by a whale
2. **Nineveh**: wicked capital city of Assyria
3. **Joppa**: port city of Israel
4. **cast lots**: the process of drawing names to identify a person by chance; "drawing straws"

MEMORY VERSE

> **MICAH 6:8**
>
> *What doth the Lord require of thee, but to do justly, and to love mercy, and to walk humbly with thy God?*

1. What are God's requirements of man?
   God requires all men to be just and merciful and to live in a way that recognizes the Lord as God.

2. What does it mean to "do justly"?
   It means to live out justice and to model fairness, goodness, and virtue in everything you do.

3. What is the nature of mercy?
   Mercy is a result of charity, compassion, and grace.

4. What does it mean to "walk humbly"?
   In all things, one acknowledges that God is the creator and sustainer of His world, and thus He is always in control. Therefore, we should live our lives in full recognition of that fact.

94   Lesson 25: Jonah | A Vision of Days to Come

From the story of Jonah, we can learn a valuable lesson. If we would desire God's grace to be freely poured out in our lives, we must freely offer this grace to others.

The story of this lesson is as follows:

- The Lord commands Jonah to go preach in Nineveh.
- Jonah flees to Joppa and boards a ship bound for Tarshish.
- The Lord sends a great wind that puts the ship in danger.
- It comes to light that Jonah is the reason, and the sailors finally (after attempting other ways) throw him into the sea, so that the sea stops raging.
- The Lord has prepared a great fish to swallow Jonah, and he stays in the fish three days and nights, when at last he is vomited onto land.
- The Lord again commands Jonah to preach in Nineveh, and when he does, the people repent.
- Jonah is displeased and wants to die.
- God makes a gourd grow to shade Jonah from the heat, and it eases his grief. But a worm destroys it, so he again longs to die.
- God asks Jonah if He should not spare Nineveh, which He made, since Jonah had pity on the gourd he had not made.

COMPREHENSION QUESTIONS

1. What order did God give Jonah? <u>God instructed Jonah to go to the sinful city of Nineveh</u> <u>and preach there. (p. 334)</u>

2. How did Jonah respond to God's command, and how did God reveal that Jonah could not hide from Him? <u>Instead of obeying, Jonah fled and took a ship in the opposite direction of Nineveh.</u> <u>God sent a great wind and storm to stop the ship. (p. 334)</u>

3. How did Jonah save the sailors from the wild sea? <u>Knowing that God was punishing him,</u> <u>Jonah allowed himself to be cast overboard to save the ship. (p. 335)</u>

4. What happened to Jonah after he was thrown overboard? How was Jonah saved? <u>Jonah was swallowed by a whale, but he prayed to God and eventually the whale spat him out. (p. 338)</u>

5. How did God reward the people of Nineveh for their repentance? What did Jonah think of it? <u>The Lord repented of His anger toward the people of Nineveh and spared them from His judgment. Jonah was angry with God for showing the Ninevites mercy. (pp. 339-341)</u>

6. The last of the prophets foresaw an expansion of God's people. Who would this future expansion include? <u>The prophets looked forward to the time when God would call all the nations to worship Him. Thus, God's people would include non-Jews also. (p. 342)</u>

GEOGRAPHY

1. Identify the important places from Jonah's story:
   ☐ Joppa
   ☐ Nineveh

BIG PICTURE OF THE BIBLE

- **Luke 11:29-32:** What did Jesus say about the sign of Jonah, and how did he contrast the Ninevites with the generation of his day?
- **Luke 15:11-32:** Read Jesus' parable of the prodigal son. Who resembles Jonah in this parable?
- **Matthew 22:37-40:** How does Jesus' answer to the question "Which is the greatest commandment?" closely resemble the spirit of Micah 6:8?

GEOGRAPHY

- Jonah went to **Joppa**, a port city on the northern Mediterranean coast of **Israel**, in order to board a ship away from God's call.
- **Nineveh** was situated beside the northern end of the **Tigris River**.

VOCABULARY AND EXPRESSIONS

1. **tempest**: powerful storm (related to Latin *tempus*, "season")
2. **"In forty days Nineveh will be overthrown."**: Jonah's brief but effective word of warning to Nineveh; the prophet gave the shortest and most poorly delivered sermon of judgment he could, but the people took it to heart. The Scripture records only this brief word to show how little Jonah wanted to fulfill the mission.
3. **gourd**: probably a tall, leafy vine that provided shade

ACTIVITIES

- pp. 334-335: What is going on in this picture? Identify the prophet. Where is this dock located?
  As Jonah the prophet boards, the crew is preparing the ship for voyage in the dock at Joppa.

- pp. 336-337: Describe the ship's appearance, possible origin, and transport system.
  The ship is a large trading ship, probably Greek or Phoenician in origin, propelled by both sails and rowers.

- pp. 340-341: Identify Jonah. What is the city in the background? What has God sent for Jonah's protection from the sun?
  With Nineveh in the background, Jonah is resting under the shade of a great gourd plant.

- p. 342: Name the instruments of war and the tools of farming.
  We see a sword and dagger alongside a plow, scythe, hoe, and pruning hook.

REVIEW LESSON: Unit 5

BACKGROUND AND SUMMARY

Use the Review Lesson to support mastery of the material presented in the previous five lessons. Drill the Facts to Know orally or have a Facts to Know Bee. Students may also write a description next to each fact on a separate piece of paper. Places to Know should be identified on the map at the end of this lesson. Students may work independently or with the teacher to complete the exercises. A test for this unit is included in the back of this book.

REVIEW LESSON: Unit 5 (Lessons 21-25)

SALVATION HISTORY

The Exile
Babylonian Captivity
A Hebrew Favored in Babylon
Rise of Persian Empire
Prophets of the Exile

Return from Exile
First Exiles Sent Home
Temple Rebuilt
Scribe Restores the Law
City Walls Rebuilt
A Prophet in Nineveh
Visions of Days to Come

Dates to Know
586 B.C.
536 B.C.

Words to Know/Vocabulary
provinces: divisions of a region
psalm: a ritual song for biblical worship
cast lots: the process of drawing names by chance
Mene: "God hath numbered thy kingdom, and finished it."
Tekel: "Thou art weighed in the balances, and art found wanting."
Peres: "Thy kingdom is divided and given to the Medes and Persians."
edict: an official order or command proclaimed by the king
cupbearer: attendant in the royal court who oversees the king's drinks

People to Know
Daniel
Shadrach
Meshach
Abednego
Ezekiel
Cyrus
Darius
Artaxerxes
Ezra
Nehemiah
Jonah
Belshazzar
Isaiah
Medes
Persians
Nebuchadnezzar

Locations to Know
Babylon
Susa
Nippur
Jerusalem
Nineveh
Joppa

Books of the O.T.
5-12-5-5-12

Genesis
Exodus
Leviticus
Numbers
Deuteronomy

Joshua
Judges
Ruth
I, II Samuel
I, II Kings
I, II Chronicles
Ezra
Nehemiah
Esther

Job
Psalms
Proverbs
Ecclesiastes
Song of Solomon

Isaiah
Jeremiah
Lamentations
Ezekiel
Daniel

Hosea
Joel
Amos
Obadiah
Jonah
Micah
Nahum
Habakkuk
Zephaniah
Haggai
Zechariah
Malachi

Give the corresponding word or phrase:

1. He was the king of Babylon that brought about Judah's exile. __Nebuchadnezzer__

2. Hebrew children that were thrown in the fiery furnace __Shadrach, Meshach, Abednego__

3. He appeared in the furnace with the Hebrew boys. __"one like a son of man"__

4. He could read the writing on Babylon's wall. __Daniel__

5. God judged this king with the words: "Mene, Mene, Tekel, Uphrarsin." __Belshazzar__

6. the next great empire after Babylon __Medes and Persians__

7. He survived the lions' den. __Daniel__

8. This Median king decreed that everyone should respect Daniel's God. __Darius__

9. priest who prophesied for God to the exiles in Babylon __Ezekiel__

10. "Now in the first year of __Cyrus__ king of Persia, that the word of the Lord by the mouth of Jeremiah might be fulfilled."

11. great prophet that foresaw both God's judgment and restoration __Isaiah__

12. The first exiles returned to Jerusalem in __536 B.C.__

13. Persian king that released Ezra and Nehemiah to return __Artaxerxes__

14. the scribe and priest that restored the Law again __Ezra__

15. the royal cupbearer who oversaw the reconstruction on Jerusalem's walls __Nehemiah__

16. Ezra read this to the people in the land. __the Law of Moses__

17. "The Lord is my shepherd; I shall not want …" __Psalm 23__

18. "When the Lord turned again the captivity of Zion …" __Psalm 126__

19. "Make a joyful noise unto the Lord, all ye lands." __Psalm 100__

20. "The earth is the Lord's and the fullness thereof." __Psalm 24__

21. unwilling prophet of God to the Ninevites __Jonah__

22. "And Jonah was in the belly of the fish __three__ days and __three__ nights."

23. In the days to come, the nations will make plowshares of their __swords__

24. What does God require of man? __to do justly, to love mercy, walk humbly with God__

OLD TESTAMENT DRILL QUESTIONS

The drill questions from Christian Studies I have been compiled in the Appendix. These questions will be used in each of the subsequent study guides for Christian Studies. Continue reviewing these as the year progresses.

REVIEW LESSON: Unit 5

TIMELINE REVIEW

Review the Big Picture of the Bible, so students understand the major periods (i.e., Creation, Patriarchs, Exodus, etc.). When they understand the periods, continue filling in the Full Timeline in the Appendix and populate each period with the important people. In this way, they will associate each person with the right events. (Example: Moses = Exodus)

Match up the Words to Know:

G	1.	provinces
E	2.	psalm
B	3.	cast lots
F	4.	Mene
H	5.	Tekel
A	6.	Peres
C	7.	edict
D	8.	cupbearer

A. "Thy kingdom is divided."
B. to draw names by chance
C. proclamation of the king
D. attendant to the king
E. ritual song of worship
F. "God hath numbered thy kingdom."
G. divisions of a region
H. "weighed and found wanting"

SALVATION HISTORY TIMELINE

Put these events in the correct order.

The Exile

3	Rise of Persian Empire
2	A Hebrew Favored in Babylon
4	Prophets of the Exile
1	Babylonian Captivity

Return from Exile

10	Visions of Days to Come
8	City Walls Rebuilt
6	Temple Rebuilt
5	First Exiles Sent Home
9	A Prophet in Nineveh
7	Scribe Restores the Law

Answer these comprehension questions from the lessons.

1. Why were the Jewish children thrown into the fiery furnace? They would not bow to the statue and worship the Babylonian gods. (p. 312)

2. Why was Daniel thrown into a lions' den? Despite the king's new law, Daniel continued to show his faith in Babylon and pray to the living God of Israel. (p. 319)

3. When visitors from Judah arrived in Persia, why was Nehemiah so sad? Hearing of the pitiful condition of those who had remained in Jerusalem, Nehemiah grieved over the misfortune of his people. (p. 328)

4. What is a psalm? A psalm is a ritual song for biblical worship. (p. 332)

5. How did God reward the people of Nineveh for their repentance? What did Jonah think of it? The Lord repented of His anger toward the people of Nineveh and spared them from His judgment. Jonah was angry with God for showing the Ninevites mercy. (pp. 339-341)

REVIEW LESSON: Unit 5

MEMORY VERSES

To recite memory verses, give the first few words and let students complete the verse orally. Students may write the verse from memory, from dictation, or copy it.

Check each box if you can recite the Scripture verse from memory. Write each from memory or teacher dictation. Be accurate.

☐ Daniel 5:25-28 And this was the writing that was written, MENE, MENE, TEKEL, UPHARSIN. This is the interpretation of the thing: MENE; God hath numbered thy kingdom, and finished it. TEKEL; Thou art weighed in the balances, and art found wanting. PERES; Thy kingdom is divided and given to the Medes and Persians.

☐ Daniel 6:23 So Daniel was taken up out of the den, and no manner of hurt was found upon him, because he believe in his God.

☐ Ezra 7:27 Blessed be the Lord God of our fathers, which hath put such a thing as this in the king's heart, to beautify the house of the Lord which is in Jerusalem.

☐ Psalm 122:1, 2, 6 I was glad when they said unto me, Let us go into the house of the Lord. Our feet shall stand within thy gates, O Jerusalem. Pray for the peace of Jerusalem: they shall prosper that love thee.

☐ Micah 6:8 What doth the Lord require of thee, but to do justly, and to love mercy, and to walk humbly with thy God?

TIMELINE REVIEW

Put the following in order on the timeline below.

1. **Dates**: The Fall of Jerusalem (586 B.C.), Reign of David (1000 B.C.), Exiles Return (536 B.C.), The Call of Abraham (2000 B.C.), The Fall of Israel (722 B.C.), Divided Kingdom (931 B.C.), Exodus (1400 B.C.)

2. **Periods**: Judges, Patriarchs, Exile, United Kingdom, Exodus, Return from Exile, Prehistory, Divided Kingdom, Conquest

3. **Events**: Fall of Jericho, The Creation, Temple Rebuilt, God's Covenant with David, The Fall of Jerusalem, Ten Commandments, Elijah Defeats Prophets of Baal, The Child of Promise

4. **People**: Nehemiah, Jacob, Aaron, Ezra, Seth, Josiah, Abraham, Saul, Samson, Joshua, Jeremiah, Noah, Caleb, Elisha, Ezekiel

Date	Events	Period	People
	The Creation	Prehistory	Seth
			Noah
2000 B.C.		Patriarchs	Abraham
	The Child of Promise		Jacob
1400 B.C.		Exodus	
			Aaron
	Ten Commandments		
		Conquest	Joshua and Caleb
	The Fall of Jericho		
		Judges	
			Samson
1000 B.C.		United Kingdom	Saul
	God's Covenant with David		
931 B.C.		Divided Kingdom	
	Elijah Defeats Baal		
722 B.C.			
			Elisha
			Josiah
586 B.C.	The Fall of Jerusalem		Jeremiah
		Exile	Ezekiel
536 B.C.		Exiles Return	
	Temple Rebuilt		Ezra and Nehemiah

MORE TIMELINE REVIEW

We cannot overstate the importance of each student truly understanding the Old Testament chronology. The Bible is God's story and, as a story, sequence is very important!

We have included here a big picture practice timeline. Continue to help students identify the storyline based on the dates, periods, events, and important people.

BOOKS OF THE OLD TESTAMENT

The Books of Law

1. Genesis
2. Exodus
3. Leviticus
4. Numbers
5. Deuteronomy

The Books of History

1. Joshua
2. Judges
3. Ruth
4. I Samuel
5. II Samuel
6. I Kings
7. II Kings
8. I Chronicles
9. II Chronicles
10. Ezra
11. Nehemiah
12. Esther

The Books of Wisdom

1. Job
2. Psalms
3. Proverbs
4. Ecclesiastes
5. Song of Solomon

The Books of the Major Prophets

1. Isaiah
2. Jeremiah
3. Lamentations
4. Ezekiel
5. Daniel

The Books of the Minor Prophets

1. Hosea
2. Joel
3. Amos
4. Obadiah
5. Jonah
6. Micah
7. Nahum
8. Habakkuk
9. Zephaniah
10. Haggai
11. Zechariah
12. Malachi

REVIEW: WHO SAID THAT?

1. "You come at me with a sword and with a spear and with a shield, but I come to you in the name of the Lord of hosts." _____ David _____

2. "Behold, the half was not told me." _____ Queen of Sheba _____

3. "I have heard your voice in the garden … I was afraid, and I hid myself." _____ Adam _____

4. "The Lord God of heaven has charged me to build him a house at Jerusalem." _____ Cyrus _____

5. "The Lord has torn the kingdom of Israel from you today." _____ Samuel _____

6. "Sun, stand still above Gibeon, and moon, stay above the valley of Ajalon." _____ Joshua _____

7. "I will celebrate before the Lord. I will become more undignified than this." _____ David _____

8. "Here I am, send me." _____ Isaiah _____

9. "Cry aloud, for he is a god … perhaps he is asleep and must be awakened." _____ Elijah _____

10. "Thou art the man!" _____ Nathan _____

11. "I will establish the throne of his kingdom forever." _____ God to David _____

12. "Fear not, and be not dismayed." _____ Joshua _____

13. "The sword of the Lord and of Gideon!" _____ Gideon's mighty men _____

14. "We want a king like all the other nations." _____ elders of Israel _____

15. "For whither thou goest, I will go." _____ Ruth _____

16. "Out of the eater came forth meat, out of the strong came forth sweetness." _____ Samson _____

17. "I am that I am." _____ God _____

18. "God will provide a lamb." _____ Abraham _____

19. "Therefore, choose life, that both thou and thy seed may live." _____ Moses _____

20. "I shall go to him, but he cannot return to me." _____ David _____

21. "Let a double portion of your spirit be upon me." _____ Elisha _____

22. "Give, therefore to your servant an understanding heart …" _____ Solomon _____

23. "Why should I not grieve since my home city, the grave of my ancestors, is laid waste and its gates consumed with fire?" _____ Nehemiah _____

24. "What means then this bleating of sheep and lowing of oxen which I hear?" _____ Samuel _____

MAP WORK

Places to Know

☐ Babylon   ☐ Jerusalem

☐ Nineveh   ☐ Joppa

☐ Nippur   ☐ Susa

We recommend that the student first locate and highlight the place to know on the labeled map, then find it and add place names to the blank map during a geography test or drill.

UNIT 5 MAP A

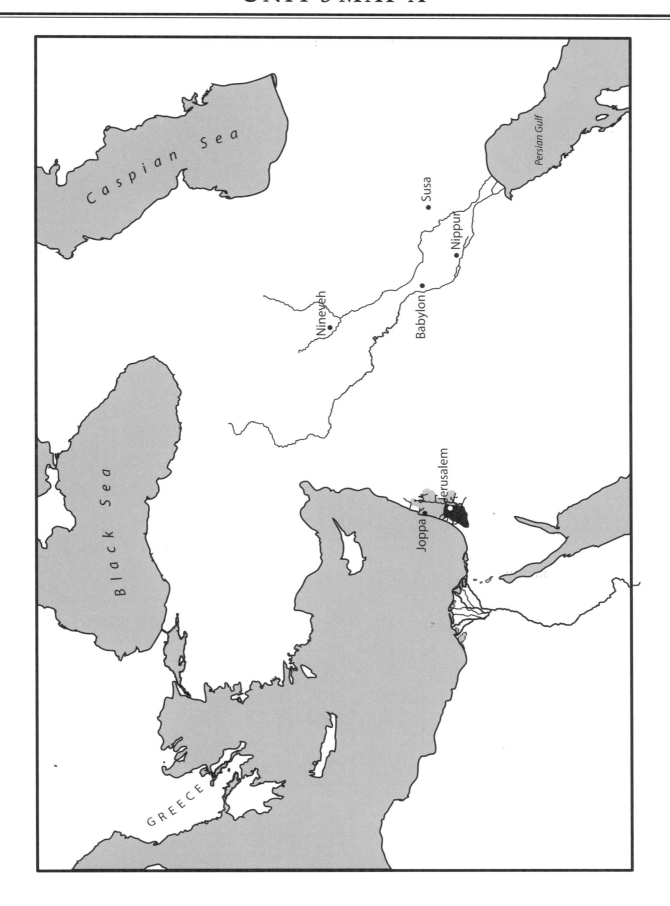

Caspian Sea

Persian Gulf

Susa

Nippur

Babylon

Nineveh

Black Sea

Jerusalem

Joppa

GREECE

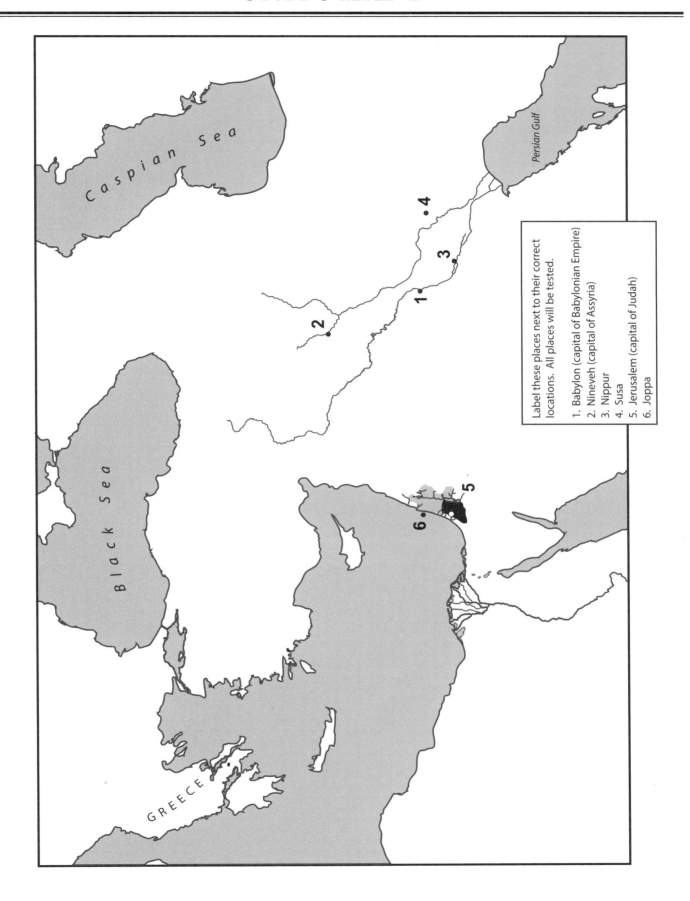

Label these places next to their correct locations. All places will be tested.

1. Babylon (capital of Babylonian Empire)
2. Nineveh (capital of Assyria)
3. Nippur
4. Susa
5. Jerusalem (capital of Judah)
6. Joppa

APPENDIX

COPYBOOK VERSES
Do you remember these verses?

1. In the beginning God created the Heaven and the Earth. And the Earth was without form, and void; and darkness was upon the face of the deep. And the Spirit of God moved upon the face of the waters. And God said, Let there be light: and there was light. And God saw the light, that it was good: and God divided the light from the darkness. And God called the light Day, and the darkness he called Night. And the evening and the morning were the first day. Genesis 1:1-5

2. And God made two great lights; the greater light to rule the day, and the lesser light to rule the night: he made the stars also. Genesis 1:16

3. And God saw every thing that he had made, and behold, it was very good. Genesis 1:31

4. And the Lord God formed man of the dust of the ground, and breathed into his nostrils the breath of life; and man became a living soul. Genesis 2:7

5. And the Lord God planted a garden eastward in Eden. Genesis 2:8

6. And the Lord God said, It is not good that man should be alone; I will make a help meet for him. Genesis 2:18

7. And Adam said, This is now bone of my bones and flesh of my flesh; she shall be called Woman because she was taken out of Man. Therefore shall a man leave his father and his mother, and shall cleave unto his wife; and they shall be one flesh. Genesis 2:23-24

8. Now the serpent was more subtle than any beast of the field. Genesis 3:1a

9. And they heard the voice of the Lord God walking in the garden in the cool of the day. Genesis 3:8a

10. And the woman said, The serpent beguiled me, and I did eat. Genesis 3:13

11. And Adam called his wife's name Eve, because she was the mother of all living. Genesis 3:20

12. Abel was a keeper of sheep, but Cain was a tiller of the ground. Genesis 4:2

13. Am I my brother's keeper? Genesis 4:9

14. But Noah found grace in the eyes of the Lord. Noah was a just man and perfect in his generation, and Noah walked with God. And Noah begat three sons, Shem, Ham, and Japheth. Genesis 6:8-10

15. Make thee an ark of gopher wood. Genesis 6:14a

16. And the rain was upon the earth forty days and forty nights. Genesis 7:12

17. I do set my bow in the cloud, and it shall be for a token of a covenant between me and the earth. Genesis 9:13

18. Thy name shall be called Abraham, for a father of many nations have I made thee. Genesis 17:5

19. The voice is Jacob's voice, but the hands are the hands of Esau. Genesis 27:22

20. And they said one to another, Behold, this dreamer cometh! Genesis 37:19

21. They stripped Joseph out of his coat, his coat of many colors, and they cast him into a pit. Genesis 37:23b-24a

22. Behold, the bush burned with fire, and the bush was not consumed. Exodus 3:2b

23. I am the God of thy father, the God of Abraham, the God of Isaac, and the God of Jacob. And Moses hid his face; for he was afraid to look upon God. Exodus 3:6

24. And I am come down to deliver them out of the hand of the Egyptians, and to bring them up out of that land unto a good land and a large, unto a land flowing with milk and honey. Exodus 3:8

25. And Moses told Pharaoh, Let my people go! Exodus 5:1 (partial)

26. Behold, I send an Angel before thee, to keep thee in the way, and to bring thee into the place which I have prepared. Exodus 23:20

27. Who is this uncircumcised Philistine that he should defy the armies of the living God? I Samuel 17:26b

28. And he took his staff in his hand, and chose him five smooth stones … and his sling was in his hand: and he drew near to the Philistine. I Samuel 17:40

29. David, the son of Jesse, the anointed of God, the sweet psalmist of Israel. II Samuel 23:1 (partial)

30. The Lord is my shepherd; I shall not want. He maketh me to lie down in green pastures: he leadeth me beside the still waters. He restoreth my soul: he leadeth me in the paths of righteousness for his name's sake. Yea, though I walk through the valley of the shadow of death, I will fear no evil: for thou art with me; thy rod and thy staff they comfort me. Thou preparest a table before me in the presence of mine enemies: thou anointest my head with oil; my cup runneth over. Surely goodness and mercy shall follow me all the days of my life: and I will dwell in the house of the Lord forever. Psalm 23

31. Make a joyful noise unto the Lord, all ye lands. Serve the Lord with gladness: come before his presence with singing. Know ye that the Lord, he is God; it is he that hath made us, and not we ourselves; we are his people, and the sheep of his pasture. Psalm 100:1-3

32. A soft answer turneth away wrath. Proverbs 15:1a

33. A merry heart doeth good like medicine. Proverbs 17:22a

34. A word fitly spoken is like apples of gold in pictures of silver. Proverbs 25:11

35. Now when Jesus was born in Bethlehem of Judea in the days of Herod the king, behold, there came wise men from the east to Jerusalem, Saying, Where is he that is born King of the Jews? For we have seen his star in the east, and are come to worship him. Matthew 2:1-2

36. They saw the young child with Mary his mother, and fell down, and worshipped him: and when they had opened their treasures, they presented unto him gifts; gold, and frankincense, and myrrh. Matthew 2:11

37. You are the light of the world. A city that is set on a hill cannot be hid. Matthew 5:14

38. Ask, and it shall be given you; seek and ye shall find; knock and it shall be opened unto you. Matthew 7:7

39. By their fruits ye shall know them. Matthew 7:20

40. Many that are first shall be last; and the last shall be first. Matthew 19:30

41. For I was hungry and you gave me food. I was thirsty and you gave me drink. I was a stranger, and you took me in. I was naked and you clothed me. I was sick and you visited me. I was in prison and you came to me. … Truly I tell you, inasmuch as you have done it to one of the least of these my brethren, you have done it unto me. Matthew 25:35-36, 40

42. Watch and pray, that you enter not into temptation: the spirit indeed is willing, but the flesh is weak. Matthew 26:41

43. And she brought forth her firstborn son, and wrapped him in swaddling clothes, and laid him in a manger; because there was no room for them in the inn. Luke 2:7

44. For unto you is born this day in the city of David a Savior, who is Christ the Lord. Luke 2:11

45. Glory to God in the highest and on earth peace, good will toward men. Luke 2:14

46. Father, if thou be willing, remove this cup from me: nevertheless not my will, but thine, be done. Luke 22:42

47. For God so loved the world that He gave his only begotten son, that whosoever believeth in him should not perish, but have everlasting life. John 3:16

48. I am the bread of life. John 6:35a

49. I am the good shepherd: the good shepherd gives his life for his sheep. John 10:11

50. It is more blessed to give than to receive. Acts 20:35b

51. The temple of God is holy, which temple ye are. I Corinthians 3:17b

52. Behold, I stand at the door and knock. Revelation 3:20

53. I am the Alpha and the Omega, the beginning and the end, the first and the last. Revelation 22:13

CHRISTIAN STUDIES I VERSES

1. And God said, Let us make man in our image, after our likeness; and let them have dominion over the fish of the sea, and over the fowl of the air, and over the cattle, and over all the earth. So God created man in his own image, in the image of God created he him; male and female created he them. And God blessed them, and God said unto them, Be fruitful, and multiply, and replenish the earth, and subdue it. Genesis 1:26-28

2. And the Lord God said unto the serpent, Because thou hast done this, thou are cursed above every beast of the field. ... And I will put enmity between thee and the woman, and between thy seed and her seed; it shall bruise thy head, and thou shalt bruise his heel. Genesis 3:14a-15

3. Now the Lord said unto Abram, Get thee out of thy country and from thy kindred and from thy Father's house, unto a land that I will show thee; And I will make of thee a great nation and I will bless thee, and in thee shall all families of the Earth be blessed. (The Call of Abraham) Genesis 12:1-3

4. And Lot pitched his tent toward Sodom. Genesis 13:12 (partial)

5. But Lot's wife looked back, and she became a pillar of salt. Genesis 19:26 (partial)

6. And Isaac spake unto Abraham his father and said, Behold the fire and the wood: but where is the lamb? And Abraham said, My son, God will provide himself a lamb for a burnt offering. Genesis 22:7-8

7. ... Esau was a cunning hunter, a man of the field; and Jacob was a plain man dwelling in tents. Genesis 25:27

8. Jacob served seven years for Rachel and they seemed but a few days, for the love he had to her. Genesis 29:20

9. And Joseph said unto them, Do not interpretations belong to God? ... Genesis 40:8b

10. The seven good kine are seven years; and the seven good ears are seven years; the dream is one. Genesis 41:26

11. I am Joseph your brother, whom ye sold into Egypt. Now therefore be not grieved with yourselves, for it was not you that sent me hither, but God. Genesis 45:4b, 5a, 8a

12. And Joseph took an oath of the children of Israel saying, God will surely visit you and ye shall carry up my bones from hence. Genesis 50:25

13. Now there arose up a new king over Egypt who knew not Joseph. Exodus 1:8

14. And Moses said unto God, Behold, when I come unto the children of Israel and shall say unto them, The God of your fathers has sent me unto you and they shall say unto me, What is his name? What shall I say unto them? And God said unto Moses, I AM THAT I AM; and he said, Thus shalt you say unto the children of Israel, I AM hath sent me unto you. Exodus 3:13-14

15. And I will harden Pharaoh's heart, and multiply my signs and my wonders in the land of Egypt. Exodus 7:3

16. And when I see the blood, I will pass over you, and the plague shall not be upon you to destroy you, when I smite the land of Egypt. Exodus 12:13b

17. Then sang Moses and the children of Israel: I will sing unto the Lord, for he hath triumphed gloriously, the horse and his rider, hath he thrown into the sea. Exodus 15:1

18. Then the Lord said unto Moses, Behold I will rain bread from heaven for you. Exodus 16:4a

19. I am the Lord thy God, which have brought thee out of the land of Egypt, out of the house of bondage.
Thou shalt have no other gods before Me.
Thou shalt not make unto thee any graven image.
Thou shalt not take the name of the Lord thy God in vain.
Remember the Sabbath day, to keep it holy.
Honor thy father and thy mother.
Thou shalt not kill.
Thou shalt not commit adultery.
Thou shalt not steal.
Thou shalt not bear false witness against thy neighbor.
Thou shalt not covet thy neighbor's house, thy neighbor's wife, nor anything that is thy neighbor's.   —The 10 Commandments (Exodus 20:1-17)

20. And he gave unto Moses upon Mount Sinai two tablets of stone, written with the finger of God. Exodus 31:18

21. And the Lord said unto Moses, I have seen this people, and behold it is a stiff-necked people. Exodus 32:9

22. The Lord bless thee and keep thee: The Lord make his face shine upon thee and be gracious unto thee: The Lord lift up his countenance upon thee and give thee peace. Numbers 6:24-26

23. And all the children of Israel murmured against Moses and against Aaron. Numbers 14:2a

24. How goodly are your tents, O Jacob, and your Tabernacles, O Israel! ... There shall come a Star out of Jacob, and a Scepter shall rise out of Israel ... Numbers 24:5, 17

25. I have set before you life and death, blessing and cursing; therefore choose life, that both thou and thy seed may live. Deuteronomy 30:19b

CHRISTIAN STUDIES DRILL QUESTIONS
OLD TESTAMENT

PART I

_____ Unit 1
1. God's act of bringing the universe into existence _____ Creation
2. "Out of nothing" _____ ex nihilo

L. 1
3. Latin for "image of God" _____ imago Dei
4. Where God placed man to enjoy life _____ Garden of Eden
5. Tree that God forbade to Adam and Eve _____ Tree of Knowledge of Good and Evil

_____ 6. Most cunning of beasts _____ serpent
7. An order of angels _____ cherubim

L. 2
8. Adam and Eve's first two sons _____ Cain and Abel
9. Adam and Eve's third son _____ Seth

_____ 10. He built the ark. _____ Noah
11. How long the rain lasted _____ 40 days and 40 nights

L. 3
12. Bird that Noah sent out to find dry land _____ dove
13. Symbol of God's covenant with man _____ rainbow
14. Where God confused language _____ Tower of Babel

_____ 15. Father of many nations _____ Abraham
16. Abraham's wife _____ Sarah

L. 4
17. Abraham's nephew _____ Lot
18. Date of the Call of Abraham _____ 2000 B.C.

_____ 19. Land given to Abraham as an inheritance _____ Canaan
20. Sarah's handmaid, the mother of Ishmael _____ Hagar
21. Age of Abraham when Isaac was born _____ 100
22. Age of Sarah when Isaac was born _____ 90

L. 5
23. Two wicked cities destroyed by fire and brimstone _____ Sodom and Gomorrah
24. She turned to a pillar of salt. _____ Lot's wife
25. "He who laughs" _____ Isaac

26. What God created on the six days of Creation, and what He did on the seventh

day one:	matter, light and dark; day and night
day two:	sky; separated the waters
day three:	dry land, seas, plants
day four:	sun, moon, stars
day five:	animals of seas and air
day six:	animals and humans
day seven:	Sabbath, day of rest

Rev.
Unit 1

Unit 2

_____ 1. Isaac's twin sons _____ Jacob and Esau

L. 7
2. Jacob's dream _____ ladder with angels

_____ 3. Jacob's two wives _____ Leah and Rachel
4. Jacob's beautiful wife _____ Rachel

L. 8
5. Jacob's plain wife _____ Leah
6. The two sons of Jacob and Rachel _____ Joseph and Benjamin

_____ 7. Jacob's name was changed to this _____ Israel

	8. Jacob's favorite son _____	Joseph
	9. He had a coat of many colors. _____	Joseph
	10. Joseph's two dreams _____	his brothers' sheaves bowed to his sheaf; sun, moon, & stars bowed down to him
L. 9	11. Egyptian who bought Joseph _____	Potiphar
	12. She lied about Joseph. _____	Potiphar's wife
	13. Title for the king of Egypt _____	Pharaoh
	14. Pharaoh's servants in prison with Joseph _____	butler and baker
	15. Joseph's youngest brother _____	Benjamin
L. 10	16. Pharaoh's two dreams _____	lean and fat cows; withered and fat ears
	17. Number of years of plenty and famine _____	seven
	18. Joseph's two sons _____	Ephraim and Manasseh
	19. He sold his birthright for a mess of pottage. _____	Esau
Rev. Unit 2	20. The three patriarchs _____	Abraham, Isaac, Jacob
	21. The three patriarch wives _____	Sarah, Rebekah, Rachel

Unit 3

L. 11	1. This was found in Benjamin's sack. _____	silver cup
	2. The part of Egypt Pharaoh gave to Joseph's family _____	Goshen
	3. Jacob prophesied this tribe would rule the others. _____	Judah
L. 12	4. The great river of Egypt _____	Nile
	5. The direction in which the Nile flows _____	south to north
	6. The sea the Nile empties into _____	Mediterranean
	7. Two cities built for Pharaoh by the children of Israel _____	Pithom and Rameses
	8. After killing an Egyptian, Moses fled here. _____	Midian
L. 13	9. The tribe of Moses and Aaron _____	Levi
	10. The departure of Israel from Egypt in 1400 B.C. _____	Exodus
	11. The tribe the Israelite priests came from _____	Levi
	12. How the angel of the Lord appeared to Moses on Mt. Horeb _____	a burning bush
	13. The Hebrew name for God _____	Yahweh
L. 14	14. The meaning of Yahweh _____	"I am"
	15. Moses' brother _____	Aaron
	16. Moses' sister _____	Miriam
L. 15	17. The arc of land stretching from the Persian Gulf to Egypt _____	Fertile Crescent
	18. He was hidden in a basket on the Nile. _____	Moses
Rev. Unit 3	19. Four names for God's people _____	Israelites, Hebrews, Children of Israel, the Chosen People

Unit 4

	1. Feast celebrating the Exodus from Egypt _____	Passover
	2. Bread without yeast _____	unleavened bread
L. 17	3. The Israelites ate this with their lamb for the Passover. _____	unleavened bread and bitter herbs
	4. The great miracle God performed in the Exodus _____	parting of Red Sea

5. The two bodies of water on either side of the Sinai Peninsula _____

L. 17

Gulf of Suez, Gulf of Aqaba

6. The place of bitter waters in the Wilderness of Shur _____ Marah

L. 18

7. The children of Israel always did this when difficulties arose. _____ murmur

8. Bread that rained from heaven in the desert _____ manna

9. How Moses got water for the Israelites in Massah _____ by striking a rock

10. Moses' father-in-law _____ Jethro

11. The Israelites defeated these people on the way to Mt. Sinai. _____ Amalekites

L. 19

12. He defeated the Amalekites when Moses held up his hands. _____ Joshua

13. Mountain where God gave the Law and Ten Commandments _____ Mt. Sinai

14. Day of rest _____ Sabbath

15. Number of days Moses was on Mt. Sinai _____ 40 days

16. Sacred object that held the Law and Commandments and went before the Israelites on their journeys _____ Ark of the Covenant

L. 20

17. Throne of pure gold on top of the Ark of the Covenant _____ mercy seat

18. Figures at either end of the mercy seat _____ golden angels with wings outspread

19. Twelve sacred loaves placed on the Tabernacle each Sabbath _____ showbread

20. Seven-branch golden lampstand in the Tabernacle _____ Menorah

21. Tent which served as a portable sanctuary for Israel _____ Tabernacle

Rev. Unit 4

22. He spoke with God face to face. _____ Moses

Unit 5

L. 21

1. Idol made by the children of Israel while Moses was on Mt. Sinai _____ golden calf

L. 22

2. The Promised Land is called a land of _____ milk and honey

3. The two faithful spies _____ Joshua and Caleb

4. Because of their sins, the Israelites wandered in the wilderness for _____ 40 years

5. The descendants of Esau who refused to give passage to the Israelites _____ Edomites

6. Aaron's son _____ Eleazar

L. 23

7. God sent fierce snakes to punish the children of Israel, but if they looked on this they would be healed. _____ brass serpent on a pole

8. Israel defeated these two peoples before entering the Promised Land. _____ Amorites and Og, king of Bashan

9. Who were the Moabites and Ammonites descendants of? _____ Lot

L. 24

10. Balak, the king of Moab, called upon this man to curse the Israelites. _____ Balaam

11. It spoke to its master after being beaten three times. _____ Balaam's donkey

12. This river empties into the Dead Sea. _____ Jordan River

L. 25

13. He died on Mt. Nebo without entering the Promised Land. _____ Moses

14. Age of Moses when he died _____ 120 years

15. The major river in the Holy Land _____ Jordan River

Rev. Unit 5

16. Who said, "There are giants in the land!"? _____ the faithless spies

17. God caused him to give a blessing instead of a curse. _____ Balaam

PART II

Unit 1

	1.	He followed Moses as leader of the Israelites.	Joshua
L. 1	2.	The river Israel crossed to enter the Promised Land	Jordan
	3.	She hid spies in Jericho.	Rahab the harlot
L. 2	4.	Where the sun stood still	Gibeon
	5.	She prophesied the defeat of Sisera.	Deborah
	6.	He defeated the Midianites with 300 men.	Gideon
L. 3	7.	Gideon's good son that told the parable of the bramble	Jotham
	8.	Wicked judge that killed 70 of his brothers, save Jotham	Abimelech
	9.	They ruled Israel between Joshua and the Kings.	the Judges
	10.	He made a rash vow and sacrificed his own daughter.	Jephthah
	11.	Enemies of Israel that lived on the seacoast of Canaan	Philistines
	12.	The strongest man in the Bible	Samson
L. 4	13.	Samson killed 1,000 Philistines with this.	the jawbone of a donkey
	14.	The source of Samson's great strength	his hair
	15.	She betrayed Samson to the Philistines.	Delilah
	16.	The four major judges	Deborah, Gideon, Jephthah, Samson
	17.	Faithful daughter-in-law to Naomi	Ruth
L. 5	18.	Ruth's mother-in-law	Naomi
	19.	The great-grandfather of King David	Boaz
Rev.	20.	Four names for Canaan	Promised Land, Israel, Palestine, Holy Land
Unit 1	21.	Two books of the Bible named for women	Ruth and Esther

Unit 2

	1.	She pledged to give her child to the service of the Lord.	Hannah
	2.	The prayer of Samuel's mother	Hannah's Song
	3.	This priest of Shiloh had corrupt sons.	Eli
L. 6	4.	The last judge and a great prophet of God	Samuel
	5.	The elders of Israel wanted a king like	"all the other nations"
	6.	The son of Kish from the Tribe of Benjamin	Saul
	7.	The people's choice of king for Israel	Saul
	8.	A man after God's "own heart"	David
L. 7	9.	The son of Jesse from the Tribe of Judah	David
	10.	Instrument David played to soothe Saul	harp
	11.	Saul's son and David's best friend	Jonathan
	12.	The Philistine giant that insulted Israel's God	Goliath
L. 8	13.	David's eldest brother that told him to go home	Eliab
	14.	David's weapon of choice against the giant Philistine	a stone and a sling
L. 9	15.	David's first wife and the daughter of Saul	Michal
	16.	The general of Saul's army	Abner
L. 10	17.	The wise lady of Carmel that became David's second wife	Abigail
Rev.	18.	City where Samuel found the shepherd boy to be king of Israel	Bethlehem
Unit 2	19.	The number of times that David spared Saul's life	twice

_____ **Unit 3**

1. He told Saul that he and his sons would die in battle. _____ the spirit of Samuel
2. The year David's reign as king of Israel began _____ 1000 B.C.
L. 11   3. Sacred object David brought to Jerusalem _____ Ark of the Covenant
4. She despised David's celebrations and dancing. _____ Michal
_____ 5. God promised this to David with a covenant. _____ an eternal throne
6. God's prophet to David _____ Nathan
7. Jonathan's lame son _____ Mephibosheth
L. 12   8. When the men went out to battle, David still tarried here. _____ Jerusalem
9. The wife that David took from Uriah _____ Bathsheba
10. The general of David's army _____ Joab
_____ 11. He told David a parable about a rich man and a poor man. _____ Nathan
12. David's son that led a revolt against his father _____ Absalom
L. 13   13. This enemy of David's was caught in a tree and stabbed to death. _____ Absalom
14. David's son that inherited the throne _____ Solomon
_____ 15. This made Solomon world famous. _____ his great wisdom
16. The center of Israel's worship _____ the Temple
17. She brought Solomon questions and gifts from a distant land. _____ Queen of Sheba
18. Date the kingdom of Israel divided between North and South _____ 931 B.C.
L. 14   19. The Northern Kingdom _____ Israel
20. He was given control of the Northern Kingdom. _____ Jeroboam
21. The Southern Kingdom _____ Judah
22. He ruled the Southern Kingdom. _____ Rehoboam
_____ 23. God's prophet to Jeroboam _____ Ahijah
L. 15   24. God's prophet that called for famine on Israel because of Ahab's sin _____ Elijah
_____
Rev.   25. The descendants of David _____ the house of David
Unit 3   26. Three kings of Israel's united kingdom _____ Saul, David, Solomon

_____ **Unit 4**

1. The wicked, pagan wife of King Ahab of Israel _____ Jezebel
2. He was murdered by royalty for his vineyard. _____ Naboth
3. Elijah rode this to heaven so he never saw death. _____ chariot of fire
L. 16   4. He took the place of Elijah and saw his ascension to heaven. _____ Elisha
5. Under Elisha's instructions, he washed himself clean of leprosy in the Jordan. _____ Naaman
_____ 6. He was the selfish servant of Elisha that got leprosy. _____ Gehazi
7. This king set to punishing Ahab's family line. _____ Jehu
8. Queen of Judah for seven years after killing her family rivals _____ Athaliah
L. 17   9. King of Judah that was hidden in the Temple as a child _____ Joash
10. High priest that protected the child king from Athalia _____ Jehoiada
_____ 11. The first prophet to foretell the fall of Israel and Judah _____ Amos
12. Prophet of Israel that held out hope for God's mercy _____ Hosea
13. The year the Northern Kingdom fell _____ 722 B.C.
L. 18   14. The nation that conquered Israel _____ Assyria
15. Greatest prophet, preacher, statesman, and advisor of Judah _____ Isaiah
_____ 16. The king who received a sign from Isaiah about the coming Messiah _____ Ahaz

17. Good king who reformed Judah according to the Book of the Law _____ Josiah

18. He prophesied in Judah during the Fall of Jerusalem. _____ Jeremiah

L. 19

19. The nation that took the best people and possessions of Jerusalem captive __ Babylon

20. Year of the Fall of Jerusalem _____ 586 B.C.

21. The king of Babylon that brought about Judah's exile _____ Nebuchadnezzar

L. 20

22. Hebrew children thrown in the fiery furnace _____ Shadrach, Meshach, Abednego

23. He could read the writing on Babylon's wall. _____ Daniel

24. The seraphim sang this in Isaiah's vision. _____ "Holy, Holy, Holy is the Lord of hosts"

Rev.
Unit 4

25. The five names for the Messiah child _____ Wonderful, Counselor, Mighty God,
_____ Everlasting Father, Prince of Peace

26. The Messiah child born to a virgin _____ Jesus Christ

Unit 5

L. 21

1. God judged this king with the words: "Mene, Mene, Tekel, Upharsin." _____ Belshazzar

2. The next great empire after Babylon _____ Medes and Persians

3. He survived the lions' den. _____ Daniel

L. 22

4. Median king who decreed that everyone should respect Daniel's God _____ Darius

5. Priest who prophesied for God to the exiles in Babylon _____ Ezekiel

6. Great prophet that foresaw both God's judgment and restoration _____ Isaiah

7. The year the first exiles returned to Jerusalem _____ 536 B.C.

8. Persian king who released Ezra and Nehemiah to rebuild the walls of Jerusalem _____
_____ Artaxerxes

L. 23

9. The scribe and priest that restored the law again _____ Ezra

10. Ezra read this to the people in the land. _____ the Law of Moses

11. Royal cupbearer who oversaw the reconstruction of Jerusalem's walls _____ Nehemiah

L. 25

12. Unwilling prophet of God to the Ninevites _____ Jonah

13. "And Jonah was in the belly of the fish" how long? _____ three days and three nights

14. "In the days to come, the nations will make plowshares of their _____ swords ."

Rev.
Unit 5

15. What does God require of man? _____ to do justly, and to love mercy,
_____ and to walk humbly with thy God

FULL TIMELINE - OLD TESTAMENT, PART II

Fill out this timeline as you learn the dates. Begin with the dates and periods, then add the most important events and the most important people.

Date	Events	Period	People
		Conquest of Canaan	Joshua
	Rahab hides the spies		Rahab
	Crossing the Jordan		
	The Fall of Jericho		
	Joshua stops the sun in Ajalon		
		Period of Judges	
	Deborah defeats Sisera		Jabin, Sisera, Deborah, Barak
	Gideon defeats Midianites		Gideon
			Jotham and Abimelech
			Jephthah
	Delilah betrays Samson		Samson and Delilah
	Boaz marries Ruth		Naomi, Ruth, Boaz, Obed
			Hannah, Samuel, Eli
	Samuel anoints Saul	Reign of Saul	Saul
	Saul keeps Amalekite spoils		Jonathan
	Samuel anoints David		David
	David smites Goliath		Goliath, Merab, Michal
	Saul's wrath on David		Abner, Ahimelech, Doeg, Abiathar, Nabal, Abigail
1000 B.C.	Death of Saul and his sons	David's United Kingdom	Witch of Endor
	David brings Ark to Jerusalem		Ziba, Mephibosheth
	God's Covenant with David		Nathan
	David and Bathsheba		Bathsheba and Uriah
	Absalom's revolt		Absalom and Joab
	Solomon builds the Temple		Solomon and Queen of Sheba
	Jeroboam given Israel		Jeroboam and Ahijah
931 B.C.	Rehoboam given Judah	Divided Kingdom	Rehoboam
	Ahab and Jezebel's idolatry		Ahab and Jezebel, Naboth

Date	Events	Period	People
	Elijah defeats prophets of Baal		Elijah
	Elijah commissions Elisha		Elisha, Naaman, Gehazi
			Jehu, Joram, Ahaziah
	Israel and Syria attack Judah		Amos, Hosea, Isaiah, Ahaz
722 B.C.	Assyria conquers Israel		
	Josiah restores the Law		Josiah
586 B.C.	Jerusalem falls to Babylon		Jeremiah, Nebuchadnezzar, Zedekiah
	Babylonian Captivity	Exile	Daniel
	Daniel finds favor in Babylon		Shadrach, Meshach, Abednego
	Rise of Persian Empire		Darius the Mede
	Prophets of the Exile		Ezekiel
536 B.C.	Cyrus returns first exiles	Exiles Return	Cyrus
	Temple Rebuilt		Darius
	Ezra restores the Law		Artaxerxes, Ezra
	Nehemiah rebuilds walls		Nehemiah
	Jonah preaches in Nineveh		Jonah
	Vision of days to come		

COMPREHENSIVE REVIEW WORKSHEETS

WORDS TO KNOW/VOCABULARY REVIEW (Part I)

Match up the Word to Know with the definition:

S	dominion	AB	butler	AJ	omer
X	cunning	M	sackcloth	G	hoarfrost
AA	enmity	AG	savory	B	onyx
W	kindred	AE	sheaf	A	ephod
Z	cleave	AH	plague	Y	signet
P	score	AF	embalm	J	proclamation
U	burnt offering	AD	caravan	T	engrave
L	famine	R	midwife	K	stiff-necked
AI	kine	AC	yearn	N	countenance
O	birthright	C	enchantment	F	murmur
Q	firstborn	D	dungeon	V	sceptre
H	venison	E	timbrel	I	frontlet

A. embroidered vestment
B. a variety of quartz used as gemstone
C. magic spell
D. prison cell
E. musical instrument like a tambourine
F. to complain
G. needle-like ice crystals after a freeze
H. meat from a deer
I. scripture encasing worn for prayer
J. public announcement
K. stubborn
L. a lack of food due to crop failure
M. garment worn for mourning
N. face
O. family inheritance for the firstborn
P. twenty years
Q. heir of blessing
R. a woman who delivers babies

S. power or rule
T. to carve into a material
U. burning an animal as a sacrifice to God
V. a king's symbol of power
W. relatives, family
X. crafty or sly
Y. seal
Z. to join or unite with
AA. hatred
AB. house servant
AC. to wish for or want
AD. a train of pack animals
AE. a bundle of wheat
AF. to preserve a dead body
AG. salty or flavorful
AH. widespread, destructive outbreak
AI. cattle
AJ. one-tenth bushel of bread

WORDS TO KNOW/VOCABULARY REVIEW (Part II)

Match up the Word to Know with the definition:

G	Yahweh-Shalom	Z	shekel	A	seraphim
Y	kinsman	N	firmament	E	Pharaoh
AD	glean	U	tabret	M	lamentation
X	flax	Q	javelin	AL	exiled
C	Baal	I	prophet	AE	Zion
V	bramble	K	parable	AB	provinces
P	avenge	R	fasting	AA	psalm
AG	spoils	F	widow	AM	cast lots
AJ	hewers of wood, drawers of water	AI	altar	B	Mene
L	vow	W	still small voice	AC	Tekel
AK	Dagon	D	sackcloth and ashes	J	Peres
AF	anointed	T	leper	O	edict
H	mail	S	Immanuel	AH	cupbearer

A. angels worshiping God in heaven
B. "God hath numbered thy kingdom."
C. false god of the Canaanites
D. worn during mourning
E. a king of Egypt
F. a wife whose husband died
G. "the Lord is peace"
H. worn as armor
I. speaks for God
J. "Thy kingdom is divided."
K. a story with a truth
L. a solemn promise or commitment
M. expression of sadness
N. sky
O. a proclamation of the king
P. to inflict punishment for harm done
Q. a small spear
R. praying without taking food
S. "God with us"
T. quarantined with skin disease

U. instrument like a tambourine
V. thorny bush
W. soft word
X. plant cultivated for fiber and oil
Y. relative, family member
Z. about half an ounce
AA. a ritual song of worship
AB. divisions of a region
AC. "weighed and found wanting"
AD. to pick up grain left by reapers
AE. another name for Jerusalem
AF. ceremonially chosen
AG. goods and riches taken in war
AH. attendant of the king
AI. structure for sacrifices
AJ. bondsmen
AK. false god of the Philistines
AL. removed from one's home
AM. to draw names by chance

TIMELINE REVIEW

Put the following in order on the timeline below:

1. **Dates**: The Fall of Jerusalem (586 B.C.), Reign of David (1000 B.C.), Exiles Return (536 B.C.), The Call of Abraham (2000 B.C.), The Fall of Israel (722 B.C.), Divided Kingdom (931 B.C.), Exodus (1400 B.C.)

2. **Periods**: Judges, Patriarchs, Exile, United Kingdom, Exodus, Return from Exile, Prehistory, Divided Kingdom, Conquest

3. **Events**: Shepherd Boy Smites a Giant, Temple Rebuilt, The Fall of Jerusalem, God Provides a Lamb, The Flood, The Burning Bush, The Fall of Jericho, Labor of Love, The Fall of Israel

4. **People**: Nehemiah, Jacob, Ezra, Jehu, Abraham, Daniel, Samson, Joshua, Jeremiah, Noah, Isaac, Ezekiel, Moses, Joseph, David

Date	Events	Period	People
		Prehistory	
	The Flood		Noah
2000 B.C.		Patriarchs	Abraham
	God Provides a Lamb		Isaac
	Labor of Love		Jacob
			Joseph
1400 B.C.	The Burning Bush	Exodus	Moses
		Conquest	Joshua
	The Fall of Jericho		
		Judges	
			Samson
1000 B.C.	Shepherd Boy Smites Giant	United Kingdom	David
931 B.C.		Divided Kingdom	
			Jehu
722 B.C.	The Fall of Israel		
586 B.C.	The Fall of Jerusalem		Jeremiah
		Exile	Daniel
			Ezekiel
536 B.C.		Exiles Return	
	Temple Rebuilt		Ezra and Nehemiah

OLD TESTAMENT TIMELINE

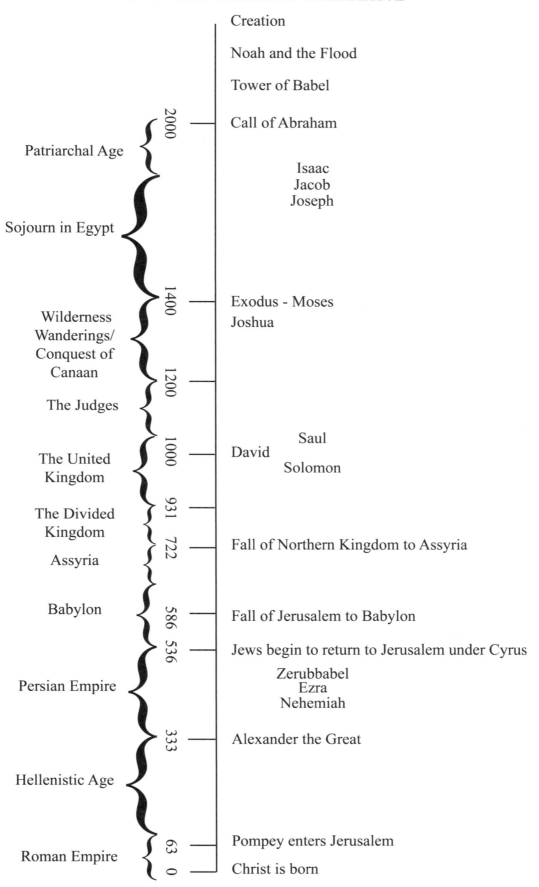

Creation

Noah and the Flood

Tower of Babel

2000 — Call of Abraham

Patriarchal Age

Isaac
Jacob
Joseph

Sojourn in Egypt

1400 — Exodus - Moses

Joshua

Wilderness
Wanderings/
Conquest of
Canaan

1200 —

The Judges

Saul

1000 — David

Solomon

The United
Kingdom

The Divided
Kingdom

931 —

722 — Fall of Northern Kingdom to Assyria

Assyria

Babylon

586 — Fall of Jerusalem to Babylon

536 — Jews begin to return to Jerusalem under Cyrus

Zerubbabel
Ezra
Nehemiah

Persian Empire

333 — Alexander the Great

Hellenistic Age

63 — Pompey enters Jerusalem

Roman Empire

0 — Christ is born

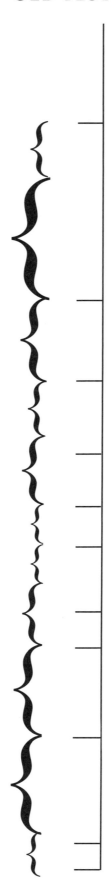

PLACES TO KNOW

Find these locations on Review Map 1:

Ai	Gibeon	Moab
Ajalon	Jericho	Mt. Gerizim
Ammon	Jezreel	Mt. Nebo
Ashkelon	Jordan River	Philistia
Bethlehem	Kedesh	Shechem
Gaza	Midian	

Find these locations on Review Map 2:

Amalek	Dan	Nob
Beersheba	Edom	Ramah
Carmel	Gath	Shiloh

Find these locations on Review Map 3:

Aram	Gilead	Phoenicia
Beersheba	Hebron	Samaria
Bethel	Jerusalem	Sheba
Dan	Mount Carmel	The Northern Kingdom (Israel)
Edom	Mount Gilboa	The Southern Kingdom (Judah)
Ephraim	Mount Horeb	Zarephath

Find these locations on Review Map 4:

Assyria	Euphrates River	Samaria
Babylon	Israel	Syria
Babylonia	Jerusalem	Tigris River
Damascus	Judah	
Egypt	Nineveh	

Find these locations on Review Map 5:

Babylon	Joppa	Nippur
Jerusalem	Nineveh	Susa

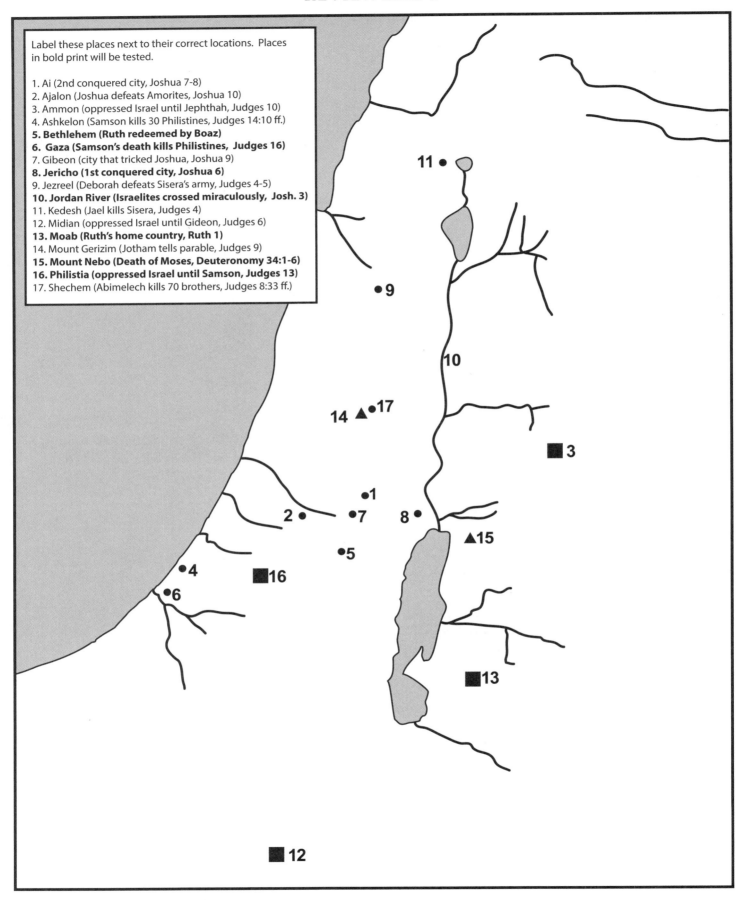

Label these places next to their correct locations. Places in bold print will be tested.

1. Ai (2nd conquered city, Joshua 7-8)
2. Ajalon (Joshua defeats Amorites, Joshua 10)
3. Ammon (oppressed Israel until Jephthah, Judges 10)
4. Ashkelon (Samson kills 30 Philistines, Judges 14:10 ff.)
5. Bethlehem (Ruth redeemed by Boaz)
6. Gaza (Samson's death kills Philistines, Judges 16)
7. Gibeon (city that tricked Joshua, Joshua 9)
8. Jericho (1st conquered city, Joshua 6)
9. Jezreel (Deborah defeats Sisera's army, Judges 4-5)
10. Jordan River (Israelites crossed miraculously, Josh. 3)
11. Kedesh (Jael kills Sisera, Judges 4)
12. Midian (oppressed Israel until Gideon, Judges 6)
13. Moab (Ruth's home country, Ruth 1)
14. Mount Gerizim (Jotham tells parable, Judges 9)
15. Mount Nebo (Death of Moses, Deuteronomy 34:1-6)
16. Philistia (oppressed Israel until Samson, Judges 13)
17. Shechem (Abimelech kills 70 brothers, Judges 8:33 ff.)

REVIEW MAP 2

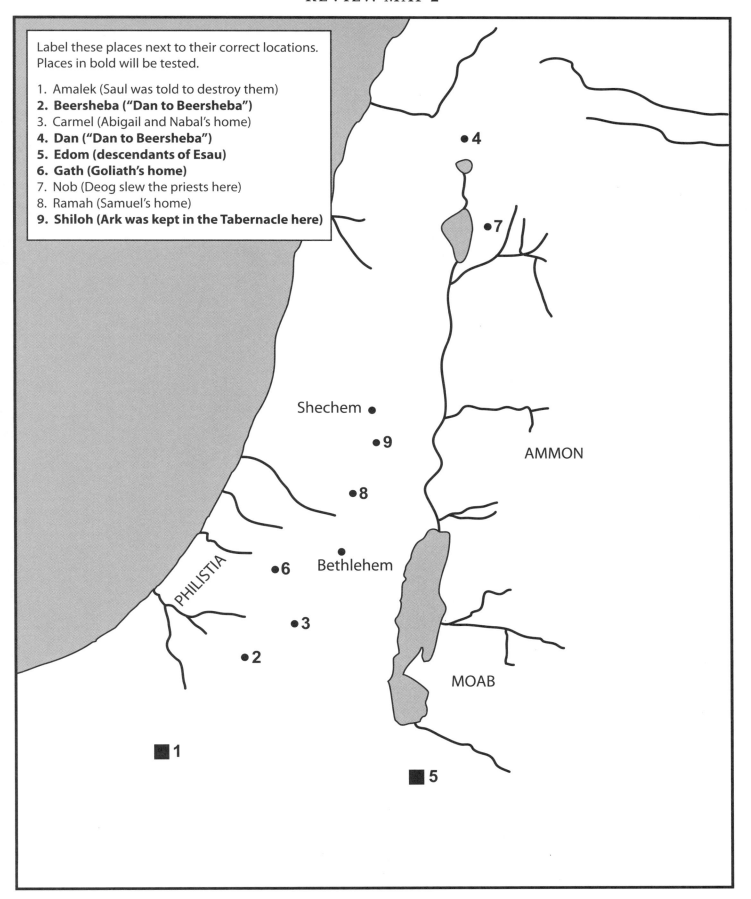

Label these places next to their correct locations. Places in bold will be tested.

1. Amalek (Saul was told to destroy them)
2. **Beersheba ("Dan to Beersheba")**
3. Carmel (Abigail and Nabal's home)
4. **Dan ("Dan to Beersheba")**
5. **Edom (descendants of Esau)**
6. **Gath (Goliath's home)**
7. Nob (Deog slew the priests here)
8. Ramah (Samuel's home)
9. **Shiloh (Ark was kept in the Tabernacle here)**

REVIEW MAP 3

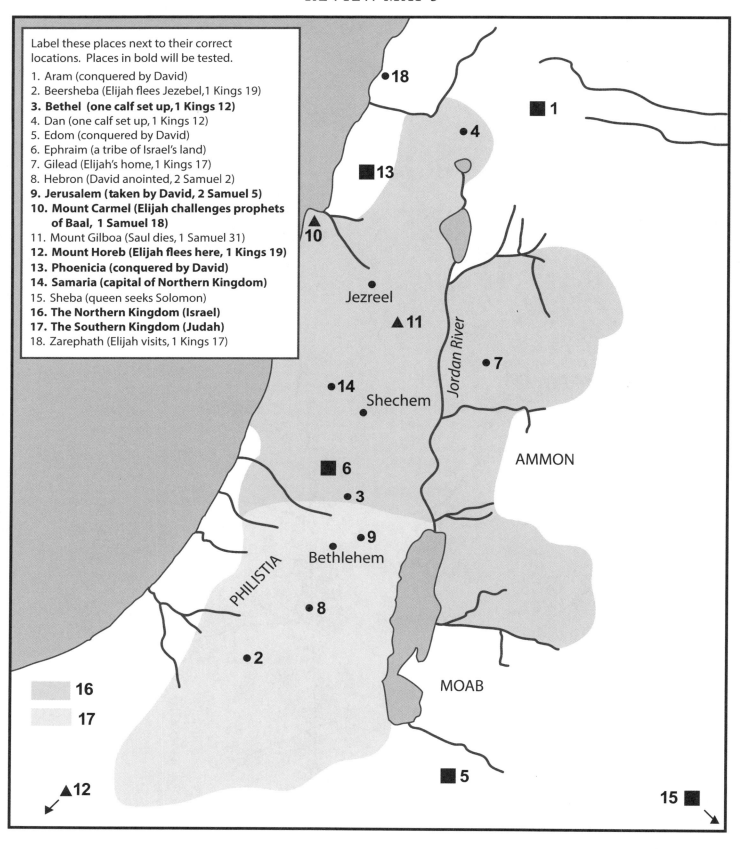

Label these places next to their correct locations. Places in bold will be tested.

1. Aram (conquered by David)
2. Beersheba (Elijah flees Jezebel, 1 Kings 19)
3. **Bethel (one calf set up, 1 Kings 12)**
4. Dan (one calf set up, 1 Kings 12)
5. Edom (conquered by David)
6. Ephraim (a tribe of Israel's land)
7. Gilead (Elijah's home, 1 Kings 17)
8. Hebron (David anointed, 2 Samuel 2)
9. **Jerusalem (taken by David, 2 Samuel 5)**
10. **Mount Carmel (Elijah challenges prophets of Baal, 1 Samuel 18)**
11. Mount Gilboa (Saul dies, 1 Samuel 31)
12. **Mount Horeb (Elijah flees here, 1 Kings 19)**
13. **Phoenicia (conquered by David)**
14. **Samaria (capital of Northern Kingdom)**
15. Sheba (queen seeks Solomon)
16. **The Northern Kingdom (Israel)**
17. **The Southern Kingdom (Judah)**
18. Zarephath (Elijah visits, 1 Kings 17)

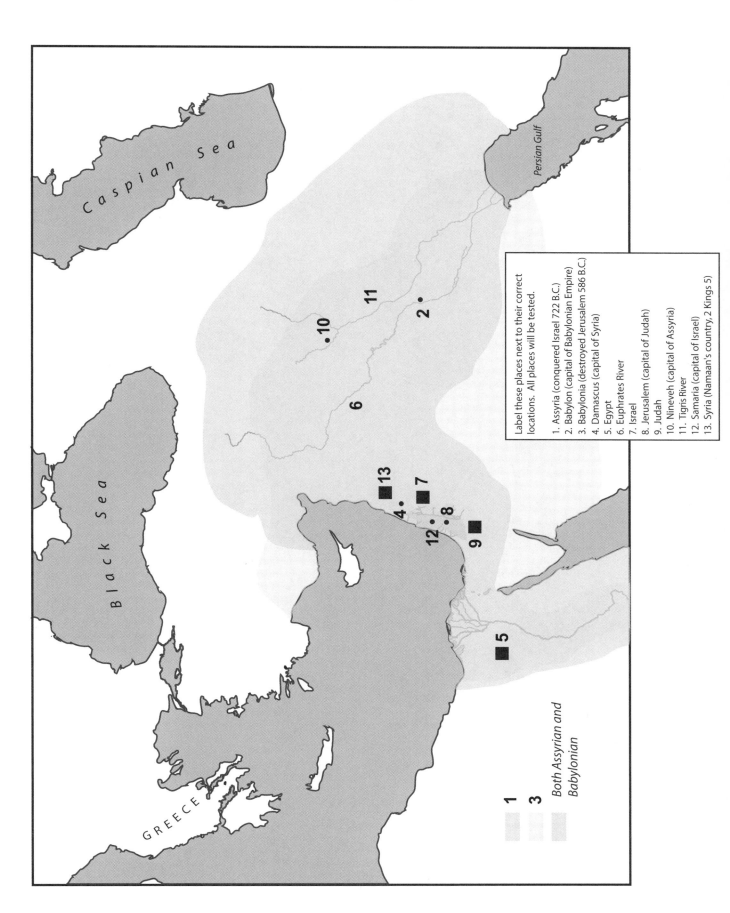

Caspian Sea

Persian Gulf

Black Sea

GREECE

Label these places next to their correct locations. All places will be tested.

1. Assyria (conquered Israel 722 B.C.)
2. Babylon (capital of Babylonian Empire)
3. Babylonia (destroyed Jerusalem 586 B.C.)
4. Damascus (capital of Syria)
5. Egypt
6. Euphrates River
7. Israel
8. Jerusalem (capital of Judah)
9. Judah
10. Nineveh (capital of Assyria)
11. Tigris River
12. Samaria (capital of Israel)
13. Syria (Namaan's country, 2 Kings 5)

1
3
Both Assyrian and Babylonian

REVIEW MAP 5

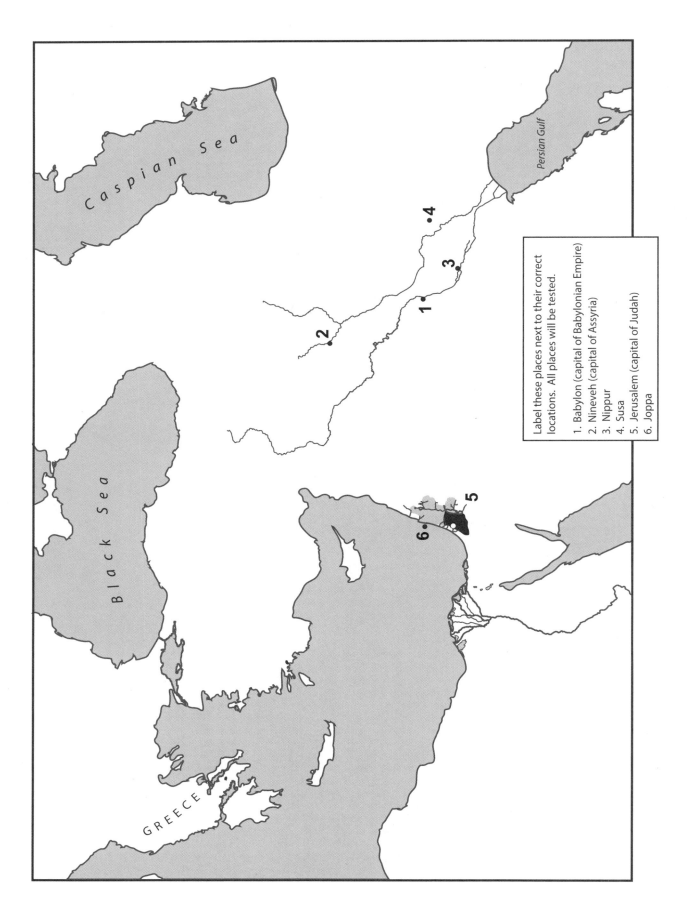

Label these places next to their correct locations. All places will be tested.

1. Babylon (capital of Babylonian Empire)
2. Nineveh (capital of Assyria)
3. Nippur
4. Susa
5. Jerusalem (capital of Judah)
6. Joppa

Caspian Sea

Persian Gulf

Black Sea

GREECE

TEST III: Lessons 11-15

Name:_____ Date: _____ Score: _____

IDENTIFICATION: Write the correct character or date in the blank next to the description. Words may be used more than once, and there may be more than one character for a description. Some words may not be used at all. (2 points each)

1000 B.C.	Bathsheba	Joab	Rehoboam
931 B.C.	David	Mephibosheth	Samuel
Absalom	Elijah	Michal	Saul
Ahijah	Jeroboam	Nathan	Solomon
Ark of the Covenant	Jerusalem	Queen of Sheba	Temple

1. Told Saul that he and his sons would die in battle: _____

2. The year David's reign as king of Israel began: _____

3. David brought this to Jerusalem: _____

4. Despised David's celebrations and dancing: _____

   God's prophet to David: _____

   Jonathan's lame son: _____

   The wife that David took from Uriah: _____

   The general of David's army:_____

   Told David a parable about a rich man and a poor man: _____

   David's son that led a revolt against his father: _____

11. Caught in a tree and stabbed to death: _____

12. David's son that inherited the throne: _____

13. Brought questions and gifts to Solomon: _____

14. The center of Israel's worship: _____

15. Three kings of Israel's united kingdom: _____

16. The date Israel was divided between the north and south: _____

17. Ruled Judah, the Southern Kingdom: _____

18. God's prophet that called for famine because of Ahab's sin: _____

VOCABULARY: Match the correct definition to the vocabulary word. (2 points each)

_____ parable

_____ fasting

_____ widow

_____ firmament

_____ Baalim

_____ altar

_____ still, small voice

A. sky

B. a wife whose husband has died

C. structure for sacrifices

D. story with a truth

E. soft word

F. many pagan gods

G. a period of prayer and self-denial

MEMORY VERSES: Write the memory verses listed below. (5 points each)

1. I Kings 10:1—"And when the_____

_____

_____

_____

_____

2. I Kings 19:11-12—"But the Lord _____

_____

_____

_____

_____

COMPREHENSION QUESTIONS: Answer all questions in complete sentences. (5 points each)

1. What did the Lord promise to do for David? _____

_____

_____

_____

2. What sin did David commit in order to have Bathsheba for himself? _____

_____

_____

_____

3. What instruction did David give to Solomon before he died? _____

_____

_____

_____

4. What did Solomon ask of God, and what was he given? _____

_____

_____

_____

5. What challenge did Elijah give to the prophets of Baal at Mt. Carmel? _____

_____

_____

_____

MAP WORK: Label the places on the map with the corresponding number. (1 point each)

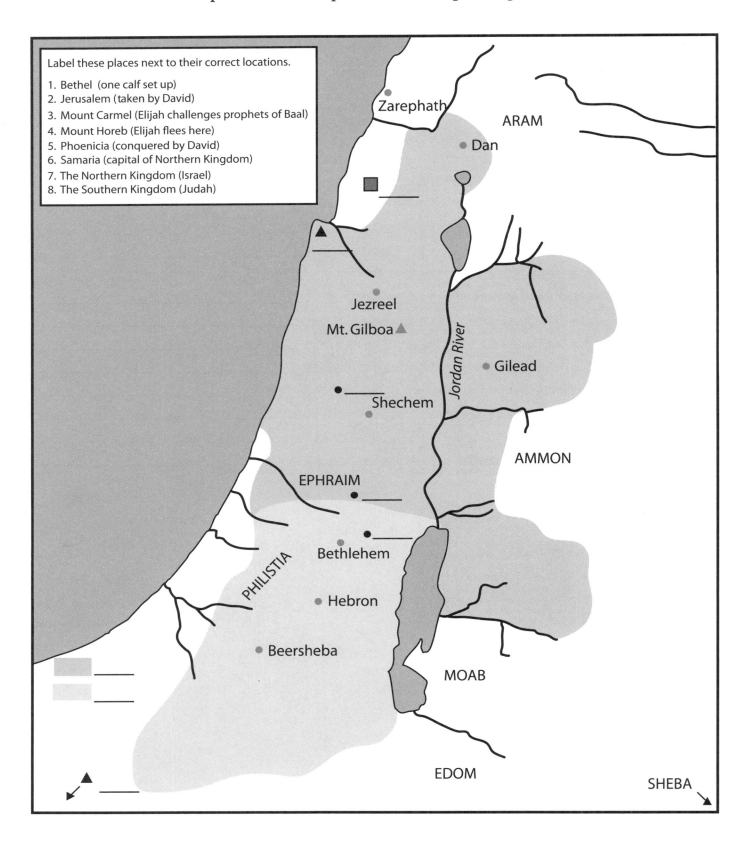

Label these places next to their correct locations.

1. Bethel (one calf set up)
2. Jerusalem (taken by David)
3. Mount Carmel (Elijah challenges prophets of Baal)
4. Mount Horeb (Elijah flees here)
5. Phoenicia (conquered by David)
6. Samaria (capital of Northern Kingdom)
7. The Northern Kingdom (Israel)
8. The Southern Kingdom (Judah)

Zarephath

ARAM

Dan

Jezreel

Mt. Gilboa

Jordan River

Gilead

Shechem

AMMON

EPHRAIM

Bethlehem

PHILISTIA

Hebron

Beersheba

MOAB

EDOM

SHEBA

TEST IV: Lessons 16-20

Name:_____ Date: _____ Score: _____

IDENTIFICATION: Write the correct character or date in the blank next to the description. Words may be used more than once, and there may be more than one character for a description. Some words may not be used at all. (2 points each)

586 B.C.	Assyria	Gehazi	Jehu	Joash
722 B.C.	Athaliah	Hosea	Jeremiah	Josiah
Ahaz	Babylon	Isaiah	Jesus Christ	Naaman
Amos	Elisha	Jehoiada	Jezebel	Naboth

1. The Messiah child born to a virgin: _____

2. The greatest prophet, preacher, statesman, and advisor of Judah: _____

3. Queen of Judah for 7 years after killing her family rivals: _____

4. Took the place of Elijah and saw his ascension into heaven: _____

5. Murdered by royalty for his vineyard: _____

6. Good king who reformed Judah according to the Book of the Law:_____

7. Nation that conquered Israel: _____

8. Nation that took the best people and possessions of Jerusalem captive: _____

9. The king of Judah that was hidden in the Temple as a child: _____

10. The wicked, pagan wife of King Ahab of Israel: _____

11. King who set to punishing Ahab's family line: _____

12. The date of the fall of the Northern Kingdom: _____

13. The date of the fall of Jerusalem: _____

14. The first prophet to foretell the fall of Israel and Judah: _____

15. Prophesied in Judah during the Fall of Jerusalem: _____

VOCABULARY: Match the correct definition to the vocabulary word. (2 points each)

_____ sackcloth and ashes

_____ leper

_____ Immanuel

_____ seraphim

_____ Pharaoh

_____ lamentation

_____ exiled

_____ Zion

A. worshiping God in heaven

B. "God with us"

C. expression of sadness

D. removed from home

E. worn during mourning

F. another name for Jerusalem

G. a king of Egypt

H. quarantined with skin disease

MEMORY VERSES: Write the verses listed below. (5 points each)

1. II Kings 2:11—"There appeared _____

_____

_____

_____

2. Isaiah 9:2, 6—"The people _____

_____

_____

_____

COMPREHENSION QUESTIONS: Answer all questions in complete sentences. (5 points each)

1. What did Elisha ask of Elijah before he departed? _____

_____

_____

2. Describe how Elijah's prophecy regarding Ahab and Jezebel was fulfilled. _____

_____

_____

_____

3. What did Amos see as the cause of Israel's weakness? _____

_____

_____

_____

4. What did Josiah do that made him such a memorable and righteous king? _____

_____

_____

_____

5. Why did Daniel refuse the king's food? What was the result? _____

_____

_____

_____

MAP WORK: Label the places on the map with the corresponding number. (1 point each)

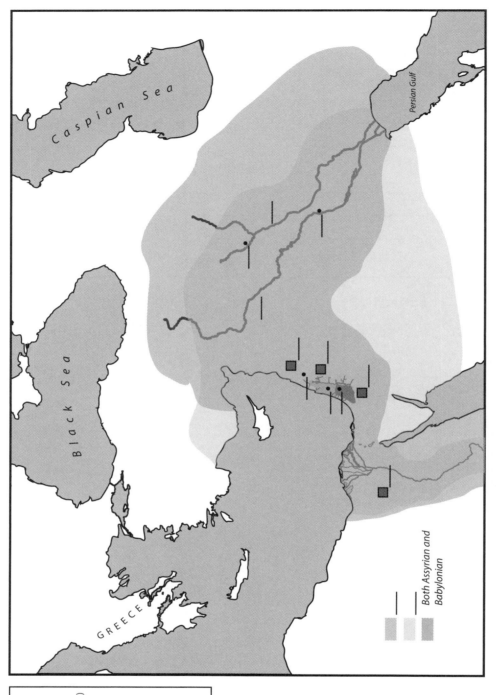

Caspian Sea

Persian Gulf

Black Sea

GREECE

Both Assyrian and Babylonian

Label these places next to their correct locations.

1. Assyria (conquered Israel 722 B.C.)
2. Babylon (capital of Babylonian Empire)
3. Babylonia (destroyed Jerusalem 586 B.C.)
4. Damascus (capital of Syria)
5. Egypt
6. Euphrates River
7. Israel
8. Jerusalem (capital of Judah)
9. Judah
10. Nineveh (capital of Assyria)
11. Tigris River
12. Samaria (capital of Israel)
13. Syria (Namaan's country)

TEST V: Lessons 21-25

Name:_____ Date: _____ Score: _____

IDENTIFICATION: Write the correct word, date, or phrase in the blank next to the description. Words may be used more than once, and there may be more than one character for a description. Some words may not be used at all. (2 points each)

586 B.C.	Daniel	Jonah	"one like the son of man"
536 B.C.	Darius	Medes and Persians	Shadrach
Abednego	Ezekiel	Meshach	
Artaxerxes	Ezra	Nebuchadnezzar	
Belshazzar	Isaiah	Nehemiah	

1. The king of Babylon that brought about Judah's exile: _____

2. Hebrew children that were thrown in the fiery furnace: _____

3. Appeared in the furnace with the Hebrew boys: _____

4. Could read the writing on Babylon's wall: _____

5. God judged this king with the words "Mene, Mene, Tekel, Uphrarsin": _____

6. The next great empire after Babylon: _____

7. Survived the lions' den: _____

8. Median king who decreed that everyone should respect Daniel's God: _____

9. Priest who prophesied for God to the exiles in Babylon: _____

10. Great prophet that foresaw both God's judgment and restoration: _____

11. The date the first exiles returned to Jerusalem: _____

12. Persian king that released Ezra and Nehemiah to return: _____

13. The scribe and priest that restored the law again: _____

14. Royal cupbearer who oversaw the reconstruction on Jerusalem's walls: _____

15. Unwilling prophet of God to the Ninevites: _____

VOCABULARY: Match the correct definition to the vocabulary word. (2 points each)

_____ provinces

_____ psalm

_____ cast lots

_____ Mene

_____ Tekel

_____ Peres

_____ edict

_____ cupbearer

A. "Thy kingdom is divided"

B. drawing names by chance

C. proclamation of the king

D. attendant to the king

E. ritual song of worship

F. "God hath numbered thy kingdom."

G. divisions of a region

H. "weighed and found wanting"

MEMORY VERSES: Write the verses listed below. (5 points each)

1. Daniel 6:23—"So Daniel _____

_____

_____

_____

_____

_____

2. Micah 6:8—"What doth _____

_____

_____

_____

_____

_____

COMPREHENSION QUESTIONS: Answer all questions in complete sentences. (5 points each)

1. Why were the Jewish children thrown into the fiery furnace?_____

_____

_____

_____

2. Why was Daniel thrown into a lions' den? _____

_____

_____

3. When visitors from Judah arrived in Persia, why was Nehemiah so sad? _____

_____

_____

_____

_____

_____

4. What is a psalm? _____

   _____

   _____

   _____

5. How did God reward the people of Nineveh for their repentance? What did Jonah think of it? _____

   _____

   _____

   _____

MAP WORK: Label the places on the map with the corresponding number. (1 point each)

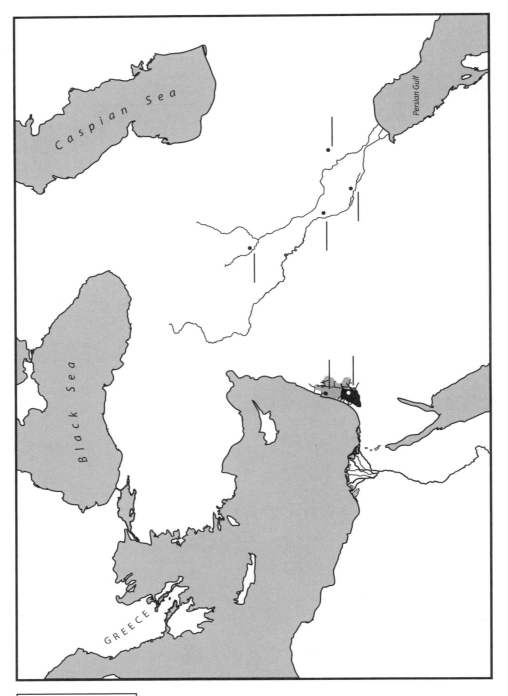

Label these places next to their correct locations.

1. Babylon (capital of Babylonian Empire)
2. Nineveh (capital of Assyria)
3. Nippur
4. Susa
5. Jerusalem (capital of Judah)
6. Joppa

FINAL TEST

Name:_____ Date: _____ Score: _____

MULTIPLE CHOICE: Circle the best answer. (2 points each)

1. Followed Moses as leader of the Israelites:
   a. Caleb
   b. Aaron
   c. Joshua
   d. Abimelech

2. Faithful daughter-in-law to Naomi:
   a. Ruth
   b. Orpah
   c. Sarah
   d. Hannah

3. Enemies of Israel that lived on the seacoast of Canaan:
   a. Amorites
   b. Hittites
   c. Midianites
   d. Philistines

4. Defeated the Midianites with only 300 men:
   a. Moses
   b. Gideon
   c. Joshua
   d. Jephthah

5. The river Israel crossed to enter the Promised Land:
   a. Nile
   b. Tiber
   c. Jordan
   d. Mediterranean

6. The strongest man in the Bible:
   a. Samson
   b. David
   c. Saul
   d. Jotham

7. Samson killed 1,000 Philistines with:
   a. sword
   b. sling & stones
   c. bow & arrow
   d. donkey's jawbone

8. Hid spies in Jericho:
   a. Naomi
   b. Hannah
   c. Deborah
   d. Rahab

9. The great-grandfather of King David:
   a. Joshua
   b. Obed
   c. Boaz
   d. Jesse

10. Ruled Israel between Joshua and the Kings:
    a. the Prophets
    b. the Judges
    c. the heads of each family
    d. the Priests

11. Two books of the Bible named for women: (Circle 2 answers for this question.)
    a. Deborah
    b. Ruth
    c. Naomi
    d. Esther

12. Betrayed Samson to the Philistines:
    a. Deborah
    b. Ruth
    c. Delilah
    d. Jezebel

13. Priest of Shiloh who had corrupt sons:
    a. Eli
    b. Samuel
    c. Isaiah
    d. Samson

14. Pledged to give her child to the service of the Lord:
    a. Ruth
    b. Orpah
    c. Sarah
    d. Hannah

15. The last judge and a great prophet of God:
    a. Eli
    b. Samuel
    c. Isaiah
    d. Samson

16. The people's choice of king for Israel:
    a. Jonathan
    b. Saul
    c. David
    d. Rehoboam

17. God said he was a "man after his own heart":
    a. Moses
    b. Joshua
    c. Samson
    d. David

18. Saul's son and David's best friend:
    a. Jonathan
    b. Saul
    c. Jeroboam
    d. Rehoboam

19. The son of Jesse from the Tribe of Judah:
    a. David
    b. Jonathan
    c. Saul
    d. Boaz

20. Where Samuel found the shepherd boy to be king of Israel:
    a. Philistia
    b. Judah
    c. Bethlehem
    d. Jerusalem

21. The Philistine giant that insulted Israel's God:
    a. Kish
    b. Eliab
    c. Attila
    d. Goliath

22. David played this to soothe Saul:
    a. harp
    b. French horn
    c. dulcimer
    d. piano

23. The general of Saul's army:
    a. Joab
    b. Abner
    c. Jonathan
    d. Mephibosheth

24. The wise lady of Carmel that became David's second wife:
    a. Abigail
    b. Hannah
    c. Michal
    d. Esther

25. Told Saul that he and his sons would die in battle:
    a. Michal
    b. Jonathan
    c. David
    d. Samuel

26. The year David's reign as king of Israel began:
    a. 510 B.C.
    b. 1000 B.C.
    c. 722 B.C.
    d. 2000 B.C.

27. David brought this to Jerusalem:
    a. Tabernacle
    b. Temple
    c. Ark of the Covenant
    d. throne

28. She despised David's celebrations and dancing:
    a. Abigail
    b. Michal
    c. Rahab
    d. Bathsheba

29. He was God's prophet to David who told a parable about a rich man and a poor man:
    a. Eli
    b. Samuel
    c. Nathan
    d. Jonathan

30. The wife that David took from Uriah:
    a. Abigail
    b. Michal
    c. Rahab
    d. Bathsheba

31. David's son that led a revolt against his father:
    a. Solomon
    b. Absalom
    c. Nathan
    d. Mephibosheth

32. David's son that inherited the throne:
    a. Solomon
    b. Absalom
    c. Nathan
    d. Mephibosheth

33. This made Solomon world famous:
    a. his riches
    b. his palace
    c. the Temple
    d. his wisdom

34. The center of Israel's worship:
    a. Temple
    b. Jordan River
    c. King's palace

35. The three kings of Israel's united kingdom: (Circle 3 answers for this question.)
    a. Jeroboam
    b. David
    c. Saul
    d. Solomon
    e. Rehoboam

36. When the kingdom of Israel divided between the North and South:
    a. 1078 B.C.
    b. 931 B.C.
    c. 846 B.C.
    d. 739 B.C.

37. God's prophet that called for famine on Israel because of Ahab's sin:
    a. Nathan
    b. Ahijah
    c. Elijah
    d. Isaiah

38. Murdered by royalty for his vineyard:
    a. Ahab
    b. Jeremiah
    c. Ahijah
    d. Naboth

39. The wicked, pagan wife of King Ahab of Israel:
    a. Abigail
    b. Jezebel
    c. Delilah
    d. Michal

40. Took the place of Elijah and saw his ascension to heaven:
    a. Elisha
    b. Ahab
    c. Michael
    d. Naboth

41. The king who set to punishing Ahab's family line:
    a. Jehu
    b. Jeroboam
    c. David
    d. Solomon

42. The captain of Syria that was cured of leprosy by Elisha:
    a. Elisha
    b. Elijah
    c. Naaman
    d. Naboth

43. Queen of Judah for seven years after killing her family rivals:
    a. Bathsheba
    b. Athaliah
    c. Jehoiada
    d. Sapphira

44. The king of Judah that was hidden in the Temple as a child:
    a. Athaliah
    b. Ahijah
    c. Joash
    d. Jeremiah

45. The first prophet to foretell the fall of Israel and Judah:
    a. Athaliah
    b. Amos
    c. Elijah
    d. Jeremiah

46. Prophet of Israel that held out hope for God's mercy:
    a. Hosea
    b. Hannah
    c. Amos
    d. Ahaz

47. When the fall of the Northern Kingdom happened:
    a. 1000 B.C.
    b. 877 B.C.
    c. 722 B.C.
    d. 634 B.C.

48. This nation conquered Israel:
    a. Assyria
    b. Egypt
    c. Philistia
    d. America

49. Greatest prophet, preacher, statesman, and advisor of Judah:
    a. Caesar
    b. Elijah
    c. Hosea
    d. Isaiah

50. The Messiah child born to a virgin:
    a. Hosea
    b. Amos
    c. Jesus
    d. Isaiah

51. Good king who reformed Judah according to the Book of the Law:
    a. Josiah
    b. Joash
    c. Ahaz
    d. Athaliah

52. Prophesied in Judah during the Fall of Jerusalem:
    a. Isaiah
    b. Jeremiah
    c. Ezekiel
    d. Nehemiah

53. This nation took the best people and possessions of Jerusalem captive:
    a. Assyria
    b. Babylon
    c. Egypt
    d. Philistia

54. King of Babylon that brought about Judah's exile:
    a. Shadrach
    b. Meshach
    c. Darius
    d. Nebuchadnezzar

55. Hebrew children thrown into the fiery furnace (circle all that apply):
   a. Shadrach
   b. Meshach
   c. Daniel
   d. Abednego

56. Could read the writing on Babylon's wall:
   a. Shadrach
   b. Meshach
   c. Daniel
   d. Abednego

57. Survived the lions' den:
   a. Shadrach
   b. Meshach
   c. Daniel
   d. Abednego

58. Median king who decreed that everyone should respect Daniel's God:
   a. David
   b. Darius
   c. Nebuchadnezzar
   d. Moses

59. Priest who prophesied for God to the exiles in Babylon:
   a. Josiah
   b. Isaiah
   c. Ezekiel
   d. Jeremiah

60. When the first exiles returned to Jerusalem:
   a. 931 B.C.
   b. 798 B.C.
   c. 536 B.C.
   d. 341 B.C.

61. The scribe and priest that restored the law again:
   a. Ezra
   b. Nehemiah
   c. Ezekiel
   d. Jonah

62. The royal cupbearer who oversaw the reconstruction on Jerusalem's walls:
   a. Ezra
   b. Nehemiah
   c. Ezekiel
   d. Jonah

63. Ezra read the law of _____ to the people in the land:
   a. Moses
   b. Isaiah
   c. Joash
   d. Jesus Christ

64. The Psalm beginning with "The Lord is my shepherd; I shall not want":
   a. Psalm 23
   b. Psalm 24
   c. Psalm 100
   d. Psalm 126

65. The unwilling prophet of God to the Ninevites:
   a. Isaiah
   b. Jeremiah
   c. Jonah
   d. Ezra

66. Jonah was in the belly of the fish _____ days and _____ nights.
   a. 3
   b. 7
   c. 40
   d. 100

67. "In the days to come, the nations will make plowshares of their _____":
   a. combs
   b. forks
   c. tools
   d. swords

Bonus: (Each correct answer worth 1 bonus point.)

1. What does God require of man? _____

2. He appeared in the furnace with the Hebrew boys: _____

3. How many times did David spare Saul's life? _____

TEST KEYS

TEST I: Lessons 1-5 KEY

Name:_____ Date: _____ Score: _____

88 pts.

CHARACTER IDENTIFICATION: Write the correct character in the blank next to the description. Words may be used more than once, and there may be more than one character for a description. Some words may not be used at all. (2 points each)

Abimelech	Deborah	Jephthah	Jotham	Rahab
Barak	Delilah	Jordan	Naomi	Ruth
Boaz	Gideon	Joshua	Philistines	Samson

1. Faithful daughter-in-law to Naomi: _____ Ruth ✗ _____
2. The strongest man in the Bible: _____ Samson _____
3. Betrayed Samson to the Philistines: _____ Delilah _____
4. Defeated the Midianites with 300 men: _____ Gideon _____
5. The river Israel crossed to reach the Promised Land: _____ Jordan ____
6. Wicked judge who killed 70 of his brothers, save Jotham: _____ Abimelech ____
7. Ruth's mother-in-law: _____ Naomi ✗ _____
8. Gideon's good son that told the parable of the bramble: _____ Jotham ____
9. Hid the spies in Jericho: _____ Rahab _____
10. Followed Moses as leader of the Israelites: _____ Joshua ____
11. Enemies of Israel that lived on the seacoast of Canaan: _____ Philistines ____
12. Made a rash vow and sacrificed his own daughter: _____ Jephthah ____
13. Ruth's kinsman redeemer: _____ Boaz ✗ _____
14. Judge that prophesied the defeat of Sisera: _____ Deborah ____

VOCABULARY: Match the correct definition to the vocabulary word. (2 points each)

__G__ Yahweh-Shalom

__F__ kinsman

__H__ glean

__E__ flax

__B__ Baals

__I__ bramble

__C__ spoils

__D__ vow

__A__ Dagon

A. false god of the Philistines

B. false gods of the Canaanites

C. goods and riches taken in war

D. solemn promise or commitment

E. plant cultivated for fiber and oil

F. relative, family member

G. "Lord is peace"

H. to pick up grain left behind by reapers

I. thorny bush

MEMORY VERSES: Write the memory verses listed below. (5 points each)

1. Joshua 1:9—"Have not I commanded thee? Be strong and of a good courage; be not afraid, neither be thou dismayed: for the Lord thy God is with thee whithersoever thou goest.

2. Ruth 1:16—"And Ruth said, Entreat me not to leave thee, or to return from following after thee; for whither thou goest, I will go, and where thou lodgest I will lodge: thy people shall be my people, and thy God, my God."

COMPREHENSION QUESTIONS: Answer all questions in complete sentences. (5 points each)

1. What was the arrangement Rahab made with the spies? How did she mark her father's house? Rahab promised not to tell the king about the spies if they would save her family. She tied a piece of scarlet cord in the window.

2. How did God assist Joshua in the battles with the Amorites? God stopped the sun and moon so that Joshua's forces could finish the fighting.

3. Why did God prevent Gideon from taking all his willing servants to battle with him? God wanted to prevent the Israelites from thinking they had defeated the Midianites on their own, without God's help.

4. How did Delilah betray Samson? _____Delilah revealed to the Philistines how to rob Samson of his strength._____

5. Who was the son of Ruth and Boaz? What was his significance in Israel?_____Their son was Obed, father of Jesse. Jesse was the father of David._____

MAP WORK: Label the places on the map with the corresponding number. (1 point each)

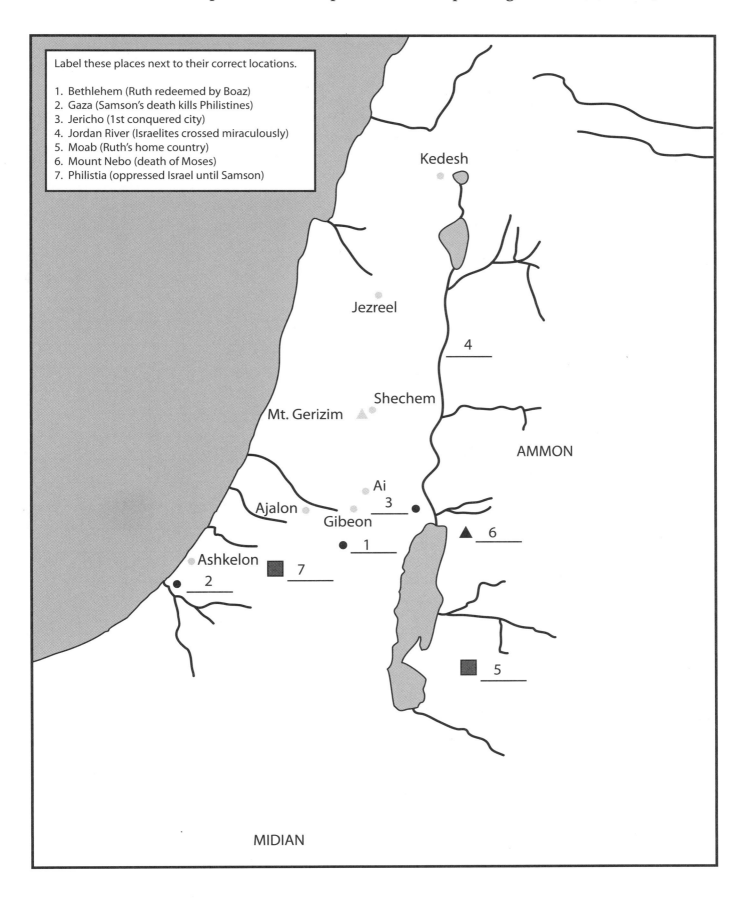

Label these places next to their correct locations.

1. Bethlehem (Ruth redeemed by Boaz)
2. Gaza (Samson's death kills Philistines)
3. Jericho (1st conquered city)
4. Jordan River (Israelites crossed miraculously)
5. Moab (Ruth's home country)
6. Mount Nebo (death of Moses)
7. Philistia (oppressed Israel until Samson)

Kedesh

Jezreel

4

Shechem

Mt. Gerizim

AMMON

Ai

Ajalon

3

Gibeon

1

6

Ashkelon

7

2

5

MIDIAN

TEST II: Lesson 6-10 KEY

Name:_____ Date:_____ Score:_____

78 pts.

CHARACTER IDENTIFICATION: Write the correct character in the blank next to the description. Words may be used more than once, and there may be more than one character for a description. Some words may not be used at all. (2 points each)

Abigail	Bethlehem	Eliab	Jerusalem	Michal
Abner	David	Goliath	Jonathan	Samuel
Ahimelech	Eli	Hannah	Merab	Saul

1. Priest of Shiloh that had corrupt sons: _____ Eli _____
2. Pledged to give her child to the service of the Lord: _____ Hannah _____
3. The last judge and a great prophet of God: _____ Samuel _____
4. The people's choice of king for Israel: _____ Saul _____
5. God said he was a "man after his own heart": _____ David _____
6. Son of Kish from the Tribe of Benjamin: _____ Saul _____
7. Saul's son and David's best friend: _____ Jonathan _____
8. The son of Jesse from the Tribe of Judah: _____ David _____
9. Where Samuel found the shepherd boy to be king of Israel: _____ Bethlehem _____
10. Philistine giant that insulted Israel's God: _____ Goliath _____
11. David's first wife and the daughter of Saul: _____ Michal _____
12. General of Saul's army: _____ Abner _____
13. The wise lady of Carmel that became David's second wife: _____ Abigail _____

VOCABULARY: Match the correct definition to the vocabulary word. (2 points each)

___F___ anointed   **A.** a small spear

___D___ mail   **B.** speaks for God

___E___ shekel   **C.** instrument like a tambourine

___B___ prophet   **D.** worn as armor

___C___ tabret   **E.** about half an ounce

___A___ javelin   **F.** ceremonially chosen

MEMORY VERSES: Write the memory verses listed below. (5 points each)

1. I Samuel 16:7—"For the Lord _seeth not as man seeth; for man looketh on the outward_ _appearance, but the Lord looketh on the heart."_

2. I Samuel 18:7—"And the women _answered one another as they played and said, Saul hath_ _slain his thousands, and David his ten thousands."_

COMPREHENSION QUESTIONS: Answer all questions in complete sentences. (5 points each)

1. Why did Hannah allow her son to be raised by Eli? _Hannah promised the Lord that if He_ _would give her a son, she would then give the child to God's service._

2. Why was David an unlikely choice for Israel's new king? _David was the youngest son of_ _Jesse, which gave him less "clout" than his brothers, as birth order was a significant_ _thing at the time. David was a young man and a humble shepherd._

3. List the many ways that Goliath had the advantage in his fight with David. What was David's advantage? _Goliath exceeded David in age, size, experience, and weaponry. But the Lord fought_ _for David, and God is stronger than even the greatest warrior on earth._

4. How did Saul's children, Jonathan and Michal, help protect David from their father? _Michal helped David escape from the palace in the night, and Jonathan warned David_ _about his father's murderous plans after he could not change Saul's mind about David._

5. How did Saul punish the priests of Nob? Why? _Saul had the city of Nob destroyed and_ _killed 85 priests because they helped David and withheld his whereabouts._

MAP WORK: Label the places on the map with the corresponding number. (1 point each)

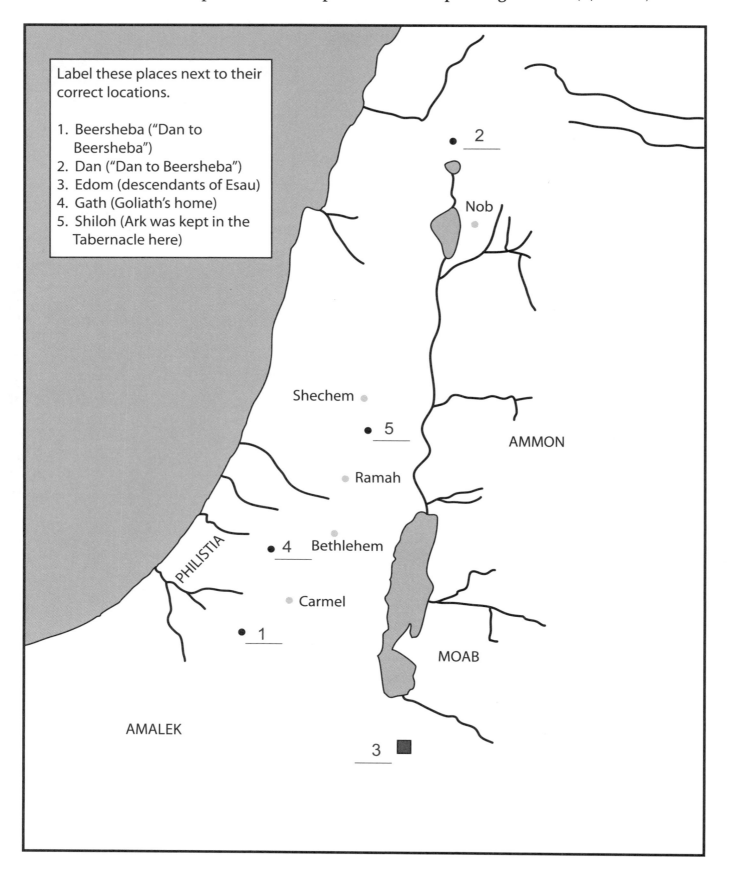

Label these places next to their correct locations.

1. Beersheba ("Dan to Beersheba")
2. Dan ("Dan to Beersheba")
3. Edom (descendants of Esau)
4. Gath (Goliath's home)
5. Shiloh (Ark was kept in the Tabernacle here)

2

Nob

Shechem

5

AMMON

Ramah

Bethlehem

PHILISTIA

4

Carmel

1

MOAB

AMALEK

3

TEST III: Lessons 11-15 KEY

Name:_____ Date: _____ Score: _____

93 pts.

IDENTIFICATION: Write the correct character or date in the blank next to the description. Words may be used more than once, and there may be more than one character for a description. Some words may not be used at all. (2 points each)

1000 B.C.	Bathsheba	Joab	Rehoboam
931 B.C.	David	Mephibosheth	Samuel
Absalom	Elijah	Michal	Saul
Ahijah	Jeroboam	Nathan	Solomon
Ark of the Covenant	Jerusalem	Queen of Sheba	Temple

1. Told Saul that he and his sons would die in battle: __Samuel__
2. The year David's reign as king of Israel began: __1000 B.C.__
3. David brought this to Jerusalem: __Ark of the Covenant__
4. Despised David's celebrations and dancing: __Michal__
5. God's prophet to David: __Nathan__
6. Jonathan's lame son: __Mephibosheth__
7. The wife that David took from Uriah: __Bathsheba__
8. The general of David's army:__Joab__
9. Told David a parable about a rich man and a poor man: __Nathan__
10. David's son that led a revolt against his father: __Absalom__
11. Caught in a tree and stabbed to death: __Absalom__
12. David's son that inherited the throne: __Solomon__
13. Brought questions and gifts to Solomon: __Queen of Sheba__
14. The center of Israel's worship: __Temple__
15. Three kings of Israel's united kingdom: __Saul, David, Solomon__
16. The date Israel was divided between the north and south: __931 B.C.__
17. Ruled Judah, the Southern Kingdom: __Rehoboam__
18. God's prophet that called for famine because of Ahab's sin: __Elijah__

VOCABULARY: Match the correct definition to the vocabulary word. (2 points each)

___D___ parable

___G___ fasting

___B___ widow

___A___ firmament

___F___ Baalim

___C___ altar

___E___ still, small voice

A. sky

B. a wife whose husband has died

C. structure for sacrifices

D. story with a truth

E. soft word

F. many pagan gods

G. a period of prayer and self-denial

MEMORY VERSES: Write the memory verses listed below. (5 points each)

1. I Kings 10:1—"And when the queen of Sheba heard of the fame of Solomon concerning
    the name of the Lord, she came to prove him with hard questions."

    _____

    _____

    _____

2. I Kings 19:11-12—"But the Lord was not in the wind: and after the wind an earthquake;
    but the Lord was not in the earthquake. And after the earthquake a fire; but the Lord
    was not in the fire: and after the fire a still, small voice."

    _____

    _____

COMPREHENSION QUESTIONS: Answer all questions in complete sentences. (5 points each)

1. What did the Lord promise to do for David? _____
   God promised to make an everlasting house for David, a line of kings that would never pass away.

2. What sin did David commit in order to have Bathsheba for himself? _____David both deceived_____
   Uriah and gave the orders that brought about the death of Uriah.

3. What instruction did David give to Solomon before he died? _David told his son that if God_
   was going to fulfill His promises to the house of David, then Solomon must keep the commandments of God found in the Law of Moses.

4. What did Solomon ask of God, and what was he given? _____Solomon requested an_____
   understanding heart that he might be a fair judge of his people. God granted him riches and honor along with wisdom.

5. What challenge did Elijah give to the prophets of Baal at Mt. Carmel? _____Elijah said both he and_____
   the priests of Baal should prepare a sacrifice but start no fire. Then they should each ask their god to produce fire.

MAP WORK: Label the places on the map with the corresponding number. (1 point each)

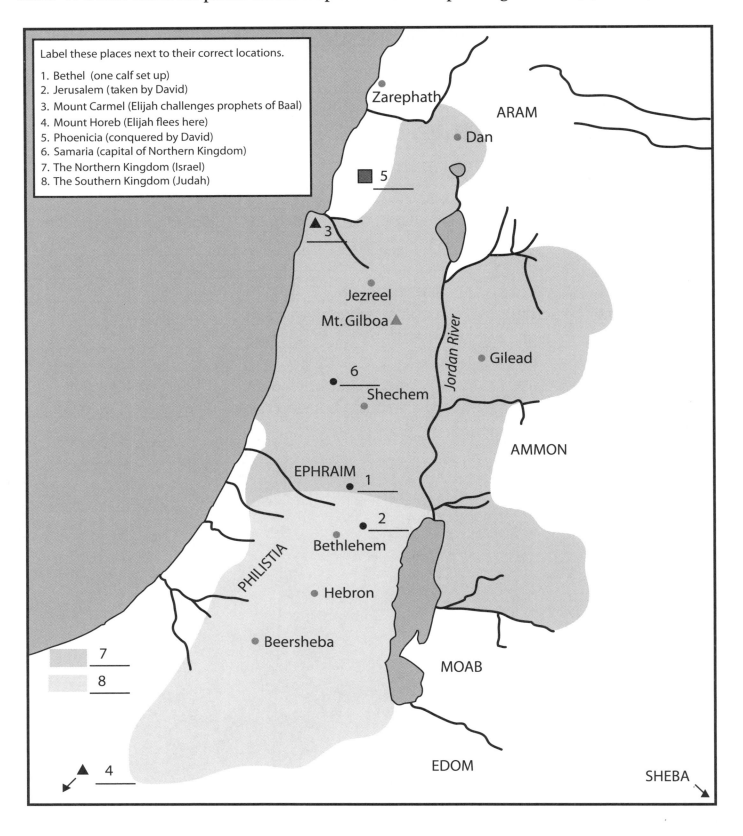

Label these places next to their correct locations.

1. Bethel (one calf set up)
2. Jerusalem (taken by David)
3. Mount Carmel (Elijah challenges prophets of Baal)
4. Mount Horeb (Elijah flees here)
5. Phoenicia (conquered by David)
6. Samaria (capital of Northern Kingdom)
7. The Northern Kingdom (Israel)
8. The Southern Kingdom (Judah)

Zarephath

ARAM

Dan

5

3

Jezreel

Mt. Gilboa

Jordan River

Gilead

6
Shechem

AMMON

EPHRAIM

1

2

Bethlehem

PHILISTIA

Hebron

Beersheba

7

8

MOAB

4

EDOM

SHEBA

TEST IV: Lessons 16-20 KEY

Name:_____ Date: _____ Score: _____

IDENTIFICATION: Write the correct character or date in the blank next to the description. Words may be used more than once, and there may be more than one character for a description. Some words may not be used at all. (2 points each)

586 B.C.	Assyria	Gehazi	Jehu	Joash
722 B.C.	Athaliah	Hosea	Jeremiah	Josiah
Ahaz	Babylon	Isaiah	Jesus Christ	Naaman
Amos	Elisha	Jehoiada	Jezebel	Naboth

1. The Messiah child born to a virgin: __Jesus Christ__

2. The greatest prophet, preacher, statesman, and advisor of Judah: __Isaiah__

3. Queen of Judah for 7 years after killing her family rivals: __Athaliah__

4. Took the place of Elijah and saw his ascension into heaven: __Elisha__

5. Murdered by royalty for his vineyard: __Naboth__

6. Good king who reformed Judah according to the Book of the Law: __Josiah__

7. Nation that conquered Israel: __Assyria__

8. Nation that took the best people and possessions of Jerusalem captive: __Babylon__

9. The king of Judah that was hidden in the Temple as a child: __Joash__

10. The wicked, pagan wife of King Ahab of Israel: __Jezebel__

11. King who set to punishing Ahab's family line: __Jehu__

12. The date of the fall of the Northern Kingdom: __722 B.C.__

13. The date of the fall of Jerusalem: __586 B.C.__

14. The first prophet to foretell the fall of Israel and Judah: __Amos__

15. Prophesied in Judah during the Fall of Jerusalem: __Jeremiah__

VOCABULARY: Match the correct definition to the vocabulary word. (2 points each)

   E   sackcloth and ashes

   H   leper

   B   Immanuel

   A   seraphim

   G   Pharaoh

   C   lamentation

   D   exiled

   F   Zion

A. worshiping God in heaven

B. "God with us"

C. expression of sadness

D. removed from home

E. worn during mourning

F. another name for Jerusalem

G. a king of Egypt

H. quarantined with skin disease

MEMORY VERSES: Write the verses listed below. (5 points each)

1. II Kings 2:11 — "There appeared a chariot of fire and horses of fire, and Elijah went up by a whirlwind into heaven."

2. Isaiah 9:2, 6 — "The people that walked in darkness have seen a great light. For unto us a child is born, unto us a son is given: and the government shall be upon his shoulder; and his name shall be called Wonderful, Counsellor, The mighty God, The everlasting Father, The Prince of Peace."

COMPREHENSION QUESTIONS: Answer all questions in complete sentences. (5 points each)

1. What did Elisha ask of Elijah before he departed? Elisha requested a double portion of Elijah's spirit.

2. Describe how Elijah's prophecy regarding Ahab and Jezebel was fulfilled. After his anointing, Jehu set to cutting off Ahab's line. He killed Ahab's descendants. On Jehu's order, Jezebel's servants threw her from the window. Jehu trampled her to death on the street and had her buried.

3. What did Amos see as the cause of Israel's weakness? _____Amos spoke out against the life of_ luxury and spiritual indifference in Israel. The Israelites enjoyed the blessings without thanking the One who blesses.

4. What did Josiah do that made him such a memorable and righteous king? _He devoted himself to_ the Lord, emptied the temples of Baal and burned their ritual objects, and he put down the idolatrous priests.

5. Why did Daniel refuse the king's food? What was the result?_____Daniel refused the food_ because it was unclean by Israel's law. He and the others ate only peas and beans for ten days, after which they were seen to be healthier than the children eating the meat and wine of the Chaldeans.

MAP WORK: Label the places on the map with the corresponding number. (1 point each)

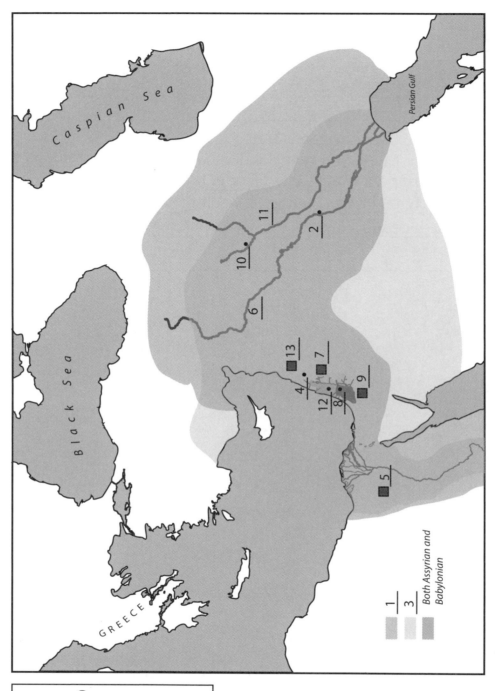

Label these places next to their correct locations.

1. Assyria (conquered Israel 722 B.C.)
2. Babylon (capital of Babylonian Empire)
3. Babylonia (destroyed Jerusalem 586 B.C.)
4. Damascus (capital of Syria)
5. Egypt
6. Euphrates River
7. Israel
8. Jerusalem (capital of Judah)
9. Judah
10. Nineveh (capital of Assyria)
11. Tigris River
12. Samaria (capital of Israel)
13. Syria (Namaan's country)

TEST V: Lessons 21-25 KEY

Name:_____ Date: _____ Score: _____

88 pts.

IDENTIFICATION: Write the correct word, date, or phrase in the blank next to the description. Words may be used more than once, and there may be more than one character for a description. Some words may not be used at all. (2 points each)

586 B.C.	Daniel	Jonah	"one like the son of man"
536 B.C.	Darius	Medes and Persians	
Abednego	Ezekiel	Meshach	Shadrach
Artaxerxes	Ezra	Nebuchadnezzar	
Belshazzar	Isaiah	Nehemiah	

1. The king of Babylon that brought about Judah's exile: __Nebuchadnezzar__
2. Hebrew children that were thrown in the fiery furnace: __Shadrach, Meshach, Abednego__
3. Appeared in the furnace with the Hebrew boys: __"one like the son of man"__
4. Could read the writing on Babylon's wall: __Daniel__
5. God judged this king with the words "Mene, Mene, Tekel, Uphrarsin": __Belshazzar__
6. The next great empire after Babylon: __Medes and Persians (combined empire)__
7. Survived the lions' den: __Daniel__
8. Median king who decreed that everyone should respect Daniel's God: __Darius__
9. Priest who prophesied for God to the exiles in Babylon: __Ezekiel__
10. Great prophet that foresaw both God's judgment and restoration: __Isaiah__
11. The date the first exiles returned to Jerusalem: __536 B.C.__
12. Persian king that released Ezra and Nehemiah to return: __Artaxerxes__
13. The scribe and priest that restored the law again: __Ezra__
14. Royal cupbearer who oversaw the reconstruction on Jerusalem's walls: __Nehemiah__
15. Unwilling prophet of God to the Ninevites: __Jonah__

VOCABULARY: Match the correct definition to the vocabulary word. (2 points each)

__G__ provinces	**A.** "Thy kingdom is divided"
__E__ psalm	**B.** drawing names by chance
__B__ cast lots	**C.** proclamation of the king
__F__ Mene	**D.** attendant to the king
__H__ Tekel	**E.** ritual song of worship
__A__ Peres	**F.** "God hath numbered thy kingdom."
__C__ edict	**G.** divisions of a region
__D__ cupbearer	**H.** "weighed and found wanting"

MEMORY VERSES: Write the verses listed below. (5 points each)

1. Daniel 6:23—"So Daniel __was taken up out of the den, and no manner of hurt was found__ upon him, because he believed in his God."

2. Micah 6:8—"What doth __the Lord require of thee, but to do justly, and to love mercy,__ and to walk humbly with thy God."

COMPREHENSION QUESTIONS: Answer all questions in complete sentences. (5 points each)

1. Why were the Jewish children thrown into the fiery furnace? __They would not bow to the__ statue and worship the Babylonian gods.

2. Why was Daniel thrown into a lions' den? __Despite the king's new law, Daniel continued to__ show his faith in Babylon and pray to the living God of Israel.

3. When visitors from Judah arrived in Persia, why was Nehemiah so sad? __ Hearing of the pitiful condition of those who had remained in Jerusalem, Nehemiah grieved over the misfortune of his people.

4. What is a psalm? _____ A psalm is a ritual song for biblical worship. _____

_____

_____

_____

5. How did God reward the people of Nineveh for their repentance? What did Jonah think of it?_____

The Lord repented of His anger toward the people of Nineveh and spared them from
His judgment. Jonah was angry with God for showing the Ninevites mercy.

_____

MAP WORK: Label the places on the map with the corresponding number. (1 point each)

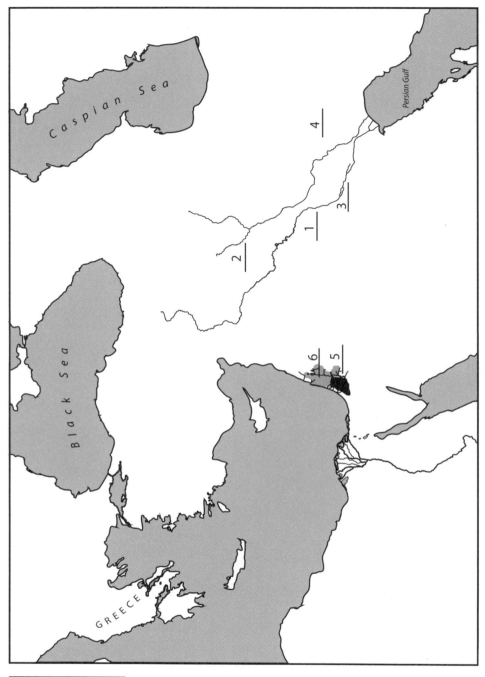

Label these places next to their correct locations.

1. Babylon (capital of Babylonian Empire)
2. Nineveh (capital of Assyria)
3. Nippur
4. Susa
5. Jerusalem (capital of Judah)
6. Joppa

FINAL TEST KEY

Name:_____ Date: _____ Score: _____

134 pts.

MULTIPLE CHOICE: Circle the best answer. (2 points each)

1. Followed Moses as leader of the Israelites:
   - **a.** Caleb
   - **b.** Aaron
   - **c.** Joshua
   - **d.** Abimelech

2. Faithful daughter-in-law to Naomi:
   - **a.** Ruth
   - **b.** Orpah
   - **c.** Sarah
   - **d.** Hannah

3. Enemies of Israel that lived on the seacoast of Canaan:
   - **a.** Amorites
   - **b.** Hittites
   - **c.** Midianites
   - **d.** Philistines

4. Defeated the Midianites with only 300 men:
   - **a.** Moses
   - **b.** Gideon
   - **c.** Joshua
   - **d.** Jephthah

5. The river Israel crossed to enter the Promised Land:
   - **a.** Nile
   - **b.** Tiber
   - **c.** Jordan
   - **d.** Mediterranean

6. The strongest man in the Bible:
   - **a.** Samson
   - **b.** David
   - **c.** Saul
   - **d.** Jotham

7. Samson killed 1,000 Philistines with:
   - **a.** sword
   - **b.** sling & stones
   - **c.** bow & arrow
   - **d.** donkey's jawbone

8. Hid spies in Jericho:
   - **a.** Naomi
   - **b.** Hannah
   - **c.** Deborah
   - **d.** Rahab

9. The great-grandfather of King David:
   - **a.** Joshua
   - **b.** Obed
   - **c.** Boaz
   - **d.** Jesse

10. Ruled Israel between Joshua and the Kings:
    - **a.** the Prophets
    - **b.** the Judges
    - **c.** the heads of each family
    - **d.** the Priests

11. Two books of the Bible named for women: (Circle 2 answers for this question.)
    - **a.** Deborah
    - **b.** Ruth
    - **c.** Naomi
    - **d.** Esther

12. Betrayed Samson to the Philistines:
    - **a.** Deborah
    - **b.** Ruth
    - **c.** Delilah
    - **d.** Jezebel

13. Priest of Shiloh who had corrupt sons:
    - **a.** Eli
    - **b.** Samuel
    - **c.** Isaiah
    - **d.** Samson

14. Pledged to give her child to the service of the Lord:
    a. Ruth
    b. Orpah
    c. Sarah
    d. **Hannah**

15. The last judge and a great prophet of God:
    a. Eli
    b. **Samuel**
    c. Isaiah
    d. Samson

16. The people's choice of king for Israel:
    a. Jonathan
    b. **Saul**
    c. David
    d. Rehoboam

17. God said he was a "man after his own heart":
    a. Moses
    b. Joshua
    c. Samson
    d. **David**

18. Saul's son and David's best friend:
    a. **Jonathan**
    b. Saul
    c. Jeroboam
    d. Rehoboam

19. The son of Jesse from the Tribe of Judah:
    a. **David**
    b. Jonathan
    c. Saul
    d. Boaz

20. Where Samuel found the shepherd boy to be king of Israel:
    a. Philistia
    b. Judah
    c. **Bethlehem**
    d. Jerusalem

21. The Philistine giant that insulted Israel's God:
    a. Kish
    b. Eliab
    c. Attila
    d. **Goliath**

22. David played this to soothe Saul:
    a. **harp**
    b. French horn
    c. dulcimer
    d. piano

23. The general of Saul's army:
    a. Joab
    b. **Abner**
    c. Jonathan
    d. Mephibosheth

24. The wise lady of Carmel that became David's second wife:
    a. **Abigail**
    b. Hannah
    c. Michal
    d. Esther

25. Told Saul that he and his sons would die in battle:
    a. Michal
    b. Jonathan
    c. David
    d. **Samuel**

26. The year David's reign as king of Israel began:
    a. 510 B.C.
    b. **1000 B.C.**
    c. 722 B.C.
    d. 2000 B.C.

27. David brought this to Jerusalem:
    a. Tabernacle
    b. Temple
    c. Ark of the Covenant
    d. throne

28. She despised David's celebrations and dancing:
    a. Abigail
    b. Michal
    c. Rahab
    d. Bathsheba

29. He was God's prophet to David who told a parable about a rich man and a poor man:
    a. Eli
    b. Samuel
    c. Nathan
    d. Jonathan

30. The wife that David took from Uriah:
    a. Abigail
    b. Michal
    c. Rahab
    d. Bathsheba

31. David's son that led a revolt against his father:
    a. Solomon
    b. Absalom
    c. Nathan
    d. Mephibosheth

32. David's son that inherited the throne:
    a. Solomon
    b. Absalom
    c. Nathan
    d. Mephibosheth

Lesson 13

33. This made Solomon world-famous:
    a. his riches
    b. his palace
    c. the Temple
    d. his wisdom

34. The center of Israel's worship:
    a. Temple
    b. Jordan River
    c. King's palace

35. The three kings of Israel's united kingdom: (Circle 3 answers for this question.)
    a. Jeroboam
    b. David
    c. Saul
    d. Solomon
    e. Rehoboam

36. When the kingdom of Israel divided between the North and South:
    a. 1078 B.C.
    b. 931 B.C.
    c. 846 B.C.
    d. 739 B.C.

37. God's prophet that called for famine on Israel because of Ahab's sin:
    a. Nathan
    b. Ahijah
    c. Elijah
    d. Isaiah

Lesson 15

38. Murdered by royalty for his vineyard:
    a. Ahab
    b. Jeremiah
    c. Ahijah
    d. Naboth

39. The wicked, pagan wife of King Ahab of Israel:
    a. Abigail
    b. Jezebel
    c. Delilah
    d. Michal

40. Took the place of Elijah and saw his ascension to heaven:
    a. Elisha
    b. Ahab
    c. Michael
    d. Naboth

41. The king who set to punishing Ahab's family line:
   a. **Jehu**
   b. Jeroboam
   c. David
   d. Solomon

42. The captain of Syria that was cured of leprosy by Elisha:
   a. Elisha
   b. Elijah
   c. **Naaman**
   d. Naboth

43. Queen of Judah for seven years after killing her family rivals:
   a. Bathsheba
   b. **Athaliah**
   c. Jehoiada
   d. Sapphira

44. The king of Judah that was hidden in the Temple as a child:
   a. Athaliah
   b. Ahijah
   c. **Joash**
   d. Jeremiah

45. The first prophet to foretell the fall of Israel and Judah:
   a. Athaliah
   b. **Amos**
   c. Elijah
   d. Jeremiah

46. Prophet of Israel that held out hope for God's mercy:
   a. **Hosea**
   b. Hannah
   c. Amos
   d. Ahaz

47. When the fall of the Northern Kingdom happened:
   a. 1000 B.C.
   b. 877 B.C.
   c. **722 B.C.**
   d. 634 B.C.

48. This nation conquered Israel:
   a. **Assyria**
   b. Egypt
   c. Philistia
   d. America

49. Greatest prophet, preacher, statesman, and advisor of Judah:
   a. Caesar
   b. Elijah
   c. Hosea
   d. **Isaiah**

50. The Messiah child born to a virgin:
   a. Hosea
   b. Amos
   c. **Jesus**
   d. Isaiah

51. Good king who reformed Judah according to the Book of the Law:
   a. **Josiah**
   b. Joash
   c. Ahaz
   d. Athaliah

52. Prophesied in Judah during the Fall of Jerusalem:
   a. Isaiah
   b. **Jeremiah**
   c. Ezekiel
   d. Nehemiah

53. This nation took the best people and possessions of Jerusalem captive:
   a. Assyria
   b. **Babylon**
   c. Egypt
   d. Philistia

54. King of Babylon that brought about Judah's exile:
   a. Shadrach
   b. Meshach
   c. Darius
   d. **Nebuchadnezzar**

55. Hebrew children thrown into the fiery furnace (circle all that apply):
    a. Shadrach
    b. Meshach
    c. Daniel
    d. Abednego

56. Could read the writing on Babylon's wall:
    a. Shadrach
    b. Meshach
    c. Daniel
    d. Abednego

57. Survived the lions' den:
    a. Shadrach
    b. Meshach
    c. Daniel
    d. Abednego

58. Median king who decreed that everyone should respect Daniel's God:
    a. David
    b. Darius
    c. Nebuchadnezzar
    d. Moses

59. Priest who prophesied for God to the exiles in Babylon:
    a. Josiah
    b. Isaiah
    c. Ezekiel
    d. Jeremiah

60. When the first exiles returned to Jerusalem:
    a. 931 B.C.
    b. 798 B.C.
    c. 536 B.C.
    d. 341 B.C.

61. The scribe and priest that restored the law again:
    a. Ezra
    b. Nehemiah
    c. Ezekiel
    d. Jonah

62. The royal cupbearer who oversaw the reconstruction on Jerusalem's walls:
    a. Ezra
    b. Nehemiah
    c. Ezekiel
    d. Jonah

63. Ezra read the law of _____ to the people in the land:
    a. Moses
    b. Isaiah
    c. Joash
    d. Jesus Christ

64. The Psalm beginning with "The Lord is my shepherd; I shall not want":
    a. Psalm 23
    b. Psalm 24
    c. Psalm 100
    d. Psalm 126

65. The unwilling prophet of God to the Ninevites:
    a. Isaiah
    b. Jeremiah
    c. Jonah
    d. Ezra

66. Jonah was in the belly of the fish _____ days and _____ nights.
    a. 3
    b. 7
    c. 40
    d. 100

67. "In the days to come, the nations will make plowshares of their _____":
    a. combs
    b. forks
    c. tools
    d. swords

Bonus: (Each correct answer worth 1 bonus point.)

1. What does God require of man? __to do justly, to love mercy, walk humbly with God__

2. He appeared in the furnace with the Hebrew boys: _____"one like the son of man"_____

3. How many times did David spare Saul's life? ___twice___